CAL
IN A WEB
OF LIES &
DECEIT

A granddaughter's
journey from victim
to survivor

LINDA KNIGHT

Cover image by: Kumo Sojo, 99D
Book design by: SWATT Books Ltd

Printed in the United Kingdom
First Printing, 2023

ISBN: 978-1-7394864-0-2 (Paperback)
ISBN: 978-1-7394864-1-9 (eBook)

Taylor Knight Books
Southampton UK

Contents

FOREWORD

I am very privileged to have been asked by Linda to write this foreword. Having been married to her for over 45 years, I know how important it is to her to tell the hard-hitting facts of her upbringing and the effect it has had on her in adulthood.

There are various types of abuse, including mental, physical, emotional, domestic, and sexual, and they all affect people in different ways.

The saying 'never judge a book by its cover' also applies to people. As an example, outwardly someone may appear quiet and be labelled unsociable or rude, but behind the cover of that person, there can be many reasons for them appearing to be that way, other than being private and reserved.

Give them time, never pre-judge and they will thank you in the end.

Sales of this book will go towards helping to prevent children from suffering abuse as well as people affected by the trauma of historical child abuse.

I am saddened that Linda is unfortunately too well qualified to write this book based on her real-life experiences, as those who should have protected her failed miserably to do so.

Linda, I truly admire your strength in getting your facts out into the public domain. I am proud of you and love you with every bone in my body.

— *Tony Knight*

PREFACE

My name is Linda Knight and I am the author of this book.

The phrase *'Faith, Hope and Charity'* sums up the reasons that the book has been written. I have **faith** *and* **hope** that this book will raise funds for **NAPAC** – The National Association For People Abused In Childhood – a charity which supports the victims and survivors of child abuse. 100% of the profits will be donated there.

The book is about three generations of the same family: grandfather, daughter and granddaughter. They have all had very different lives for individual reasons; some of their circumstances have caused them to be the way that they are as people, both then but also now.

Firstly, there is my maternal grandfather, a criminal. He is the first generation.

Miss Y is a daughter of my grandfather and is also a criminal. Additionally, she is a cheat and compulsive liar. She is the second generation.

I am the granddaughter and the third character of the three in this book, and I have reversed the trend of the first two generations.

All is not as it seems on the surface with this family, and as this book progresses, to the third part with the dark side and the very raw effect this has had on my life for many, many decades and still continues to haunt me.

It will never simply go away and it cannot be erased.

The facts in this book are based on real people and their real lives. However, for privacy reasons their names and identities have been changed whenever possible.

The places named refer to actual locations to ensure the book gives a true flavour of where the main characters were living during particular time periods.

PART ONE

MY MATERNAL
GRANDFATHER

CHAPTER 1

MY MATERNAL GRANDFATHER AND HIS EARLY LIFE

My maternal grandfather was an imposter, a fraudster, a thief, an embezzler, and a liar.

Strong charges, I know. But, as this book will show, in-depth research into my family history by myself and my husband, over many years, has unfortunately shown every one of these accusations to be true.

One thing our research has uncovered was that back in the pre-1920s era, physical proof to validate someone's identity was not needed. This hadn't yet become necessary, legally or otherwise; and as back then there were no computer records or databases, or the ability to search online, it just took the falsification of paperwork to take on a new identity.

This left things completely open to what could and did indeed happen: many deliberate cases of identity thefts.

These days it is called social engineering, but it is what it has always been, plain and simply a crime.

That is, of course, because before the 1920s, there were only manual ways of stealing the factual identity of a person compared to the research methodology of current times. After all, there was no Google or any other search engines then that is partly, amongst other reasons we will come onto, where the title **Caught in a Web of Lies and Deceit** comes from.

We didn't, and still don't, have expectations regarding what we would learn about my grandfather. Such was his life and, it seems, his use of many identities, he was a very hard character to track. After all, an imposter doesn't want to be found, nor does a fraudster, thief, embezzler etc...

And when all of these crimes refer to someone so very close to home in one's own family history, it hits very hard in so many different ways.

The research was considerably time consuming on many of these occasions and was also a painstakingly and complicated experience to deal with when working on the first character, my grandfather. It took almost three decades to discover even the very basic of facts about him. The reason for the delays in research was mainly due to the remaining members of his 'current' family in England who were unwilling to help with anything or to provide any accurate information on him.

Any "facts" they did offer turned out to be either incorrect or intentionally untrue. So, we have been reliant on patiently locating and analysing both paper documents and digital records which have been very slowly released and sourced from many and various archives and depositories.

My maternal grandfather was born and had lived in Boston, Massachusetts, USA. He was a first-generation American, as his parents had immigrated from Eastern Europe in 1890 along with several siblings that formed the rest of his family. This has been proven by checking the many American censuses partly by way of verification and additionally through DNA testing along with certification too.

My grandfather was the youngest son in the family group.

His father and one of my grandfather's siblings had both become naturalised as American citizens following their immigration and were therefore no longer legally looked upon as Eastern Europeans although they were previously regarded as having been so.

They would however, of course, remain of Eastern European and Jewish descent through their bloodline, despite their naturalisation as that does not and will not ever alter any aspect of their heritage whatever happens.

This heritage has also shown up in my genetics result in the third part of this book which relates to myself.

My grandfather, in addition to any remaining siblings and his mother would have automatically become American citizens as a result of my great-grandfather becoming a naturalised American as opposed to their Eastern European origins.

This has also been confirmed by paper records and is amongst our archived collection.

Part of this process was that his father and sibling had to *renounce all allegiance and fidelity to every foreign prince, state, potentate and sovereignty whatsoever – more especially to Nicholas II Czar of Russia.*

Neither my grandfather nor his remaining siblings had any say whatsoever in this matter at the time as they were still children.

My grandfather had deliberately and frequently lied on many occasions, at different ages, about many things, in various places and countries about his actual birth country and of his original heritage.

In the 1900 American census, he was living with his parents and his siblings in the town of his birthplace which was Boston, Massachusetts, on the surface appearing to be a normal young boy, receiving his Jewish education as part of the local community during the week and sometimes, additionally, during the evenings.

He would then have been able to play with his local friends but only when he wasn't required to help his father at the family market stall where his father was a pedlar by trade.

My great-grandfather had been a pedlar for many years – and you will see variants of this word cropping up from time to time in the second part of this book, relating to his daughter Miss Y, although with a completely different meaning altogether.

The property that had been rented by his parents during his childhood years was very overcrowded, as would be expected for a family of very limited means, tight for space and cramped for the family to have lived in, at that time. But, they made do with what they had. Many other families experienced very similar circumstances, but at least they had a roof over their heads.

The family income was very stretched as money was very limited. The address that the family lived at in Boston was identified in records from 1893, 1897 and 1898, with the house being the actual birthplace of my grandfather.

There was a suggestion from my grandfather's daughter, Miss Y, that the family was linked to the Salem witches. This proved not to be correct and so eliminated one myth; no Salem witches...

In 1899, the family moved to another address in the Boston area, where they were still located at the time of the 1900 American census.

Except for my grandfather and another sibling, the entire family were shown as having been born in Poland, although this was also shown as being part of Russia as they had effectively taken over the Polish territories and annexed it to Russia at that time.

The census also revealed that a widowed aunt of my grandfather was living nearby with some of his cousins, and a big family celebration took place in 1904 when the City records showed that one of these cousins had married at the age of 23. By this time the family including my grandfather had relocated again and then this was followed by another move in 1908 to yet another different address.

Then in 1908, a terrible tragedy struck the entire family when the father of my grandfather and his siblings (my great grandfather) contracted cancer and suddenly passed away at what was a relatively young age.

This was a very severe blow and an extremely sad and difficult time for every single member of the household and indeed, for many other people in the extended family as well.

It would have had a severe impact on all concerned, but my great grandmother would have found it extremely tough, by now having been widowed, but at least she would have had her family around her to provide the necessary comfort and support.

The reduction in the family income would have caused an even tighter financial strain than might otherwise have occurred at the time, but the family would have been able to help out in different ways.

After his father had passed away and almost certainly because of the drop in income caused by the death, yet another house move took place in 1909, to a poorer area and a location where a terrible fire was to later occur.

According to the newspaper report on the fire, it was necessary for the fire brigade to evacuate the whole family along with all the other residents of the five-storey tenement building, totalling 26 people, some of whom were adults but they mainly consisted of children. All of these residents were forced out onto the street in the early hours of a freezing winter morning, whilst they waited for the fire brigade to completely douse the flames.

Boston tenements were similar in many ways to how similar properties were in England, evidenced by the inner-city back-to-back housing that was commonplace in places such as London, Birmingham and Liverpool, with many having outside shared facilities. However, in America the properties were mainly of a high-rise type and difficult to evacuate from but also with extensive use of timber in their construction and therefore much more prone to fire.

Thankfully, in this case, the damage to the structure of the house was minor and the family were able to return again to the property and indeed, continued to live there for a further two years.

The next American census was carried out in 1910 covering the whole of the USA.

By now the family living at home consisted of my great-grandmother who of course was a widow, having lost her husband two years previously as well as any of the children and other family members who although adults by now were still living at home.

This census return showed that my grandfather was now old enough to have obtained a job, working as an errand boy for a tailoring business with other siblings also holding various other jobs so that they could help the family and were pulling together as a whole to improve their lot.

In 1911 the family had moved on again to yet another house, but still remained within the Boston city limits.

The summer of 1914 had brought more joy to the family with another family wedding especially as this resulted in the integration of two local Jewish families into each other.

However, later on in that same year, my grandfather himself moved out of the family home and went to live in Maine, the neighbouring State to Massachusetts, further up the coast. He either moved in with or was living close to another sibling, who was running a business in what was a popular seaside town of that era.

As my grandfather and any of his family became older, they gradually obtained more work or they had relocated for various reasons. As a result of this, the family numbers had reduced at the family home, where his mother had continued living with the family members that still remained in the city in 1915 and were living in a single family unit in a Boston suburb.

During these early years in Boston, there had been a certain amount of resentment from the locals, with my grandfather and his remaining family, in addition to many others in a similar position to themselves, continuing to be treated as immigrants despite by now having become naturalised as American citizens. The situation didn't improve as they were seen to be taking up very important space, property rentals and jobs where other Americans could otherwise have lived in or worked at themselves.

As my grandfather and his siblings grew up, they either worked full time or found a number of part-time jobs to enable themselves to have at least some financial income.

In addition to this they also collaborated with other members of the local Jewish community in order to assist and support each other in various ways, in an attempt to support the financial needs of the extended family that they were now part of, all pulling together as one extended family demonstrating true community support for each other.

The living conditions were much the same as the family had originally left behind them in Eastern Europe, which at the time would also have been with poor sanitation and water supplies.

One of the benefits of the immigration was that the family were no longer being persecuted for their religious beliefs as Jews, as they had been back in their homeland even if there was still prejudice of sorts.

Although space and conditions were limited overall, their new environment would still have been a massive improvement on where they would have originated from in their homeland and the suffering that would have had to be endured by them at the time and there is no doubt that they would have been treated as lower class citizens.

Health conditions were poor because of the overcrowding and the water limitations. Diseases such as cholera, tuberculosis, and smallpox, to name but a few, were rife in the poorer housing facilities at this time. From an employment perspective, the family members capable of employment would be able to learn new skills and could then move their way up the ranks, increasing the opportunities for themselves and their families and at the same time, improving on their living conditions.

They may well have also changed direction in their work for the very same reasons so as to do better and increase their chances of either promotion, their pay or simply for a different and better lifestyle.

Then from there they either found their own separate accommodation to move into eventually, possibly as a result of getting married.

There would have also been opportunities to move out of the area for their work so that there then would have been chances for them to further advance themselves either in the same jobs or even taking different careers in order to generally improve their lot.

As a young teenager, my grandfather had been good at sport, especially running and had also helped to organise other activities at school, including theatrical shows.

This should have set him in good stead, but unfortunately rather than making the most of his skills, he ran very much in the opposing direction and straight into a huge amount of trouble.

When most of the family had still lived at home prior to 1915, they all contributed their bit and had helped with the household expenses, including my grandfather himself who was by now in his mid-teens.

The 1910 American census had confirmed the work my grandfather had been doing whilst employed as an errand boy for a tailor. It would have involved tasks such as carrying large, bulky and sometimes heavy rolls of material or sewing equipment across the city from the sweatshop where his work was based to the premises of customers or suppliers. It was a learning curve and necessary to start on the bottom rung of the ladder, just as his then boss had done as a start-up job.

It really was tough work for my grandfather, working very long and tiring hours for a mere pittance of a wage and perhaps it was the financial limitations along with the loss of his father that proved to be the final straw. He may have done things differently if he'd had his father around for guidance. Having said that, he may well have received help and guidance from the Jewish community or indeed his own siblings to be steered back in the right direction. We can't know.

Perhaps it had been these circumstances that had finally tipped my grandfather over the edge and into the world of criminal activities in which he would soon be an active member. However, his situation was not a satisfactory reason or excuse for any sort for stealing.

CHAPTER 2
TURNING TO CRIME

My grandfather seemed to make completely the wrong choices and took little notice of any guidance and so did not get back onto the straight and narrow as he may well have done otherwise.

It would seem at least on the surface, that he had just been a bad boy who became exceptionally greedy at the time, in addition to probably getting into the wrong kind of company.

This is impossible to say in the circumstances, but still not the right thing to do at the time as honesty has always been the correct policy, not by using other people or by causing them a huge amount of financial hardship and certainly not by stealing from them either.

My grandfather had stolen from his first employer who was a tailor by trade as mentioned earlier and at some point before my grandfather had begun working for him, he would have been in the very same position of learning as my grandfather would have been, by starting on the bottom rung of the ladder and then would have been given an opportunity to make the most of his prospects for himself, having been given a good chance to learn a good trade.

The tailor would have employed my grandfather out of the kindness of his heart and to give him a similar opportunity that he had at the same point, to obtain valuable skills.

However, his employer's only reward would have been to have a large amount of quality cloth rolls and finished clothing embezzled from him, over quite a long period. My grandfather was heartless, dishonest and cruel, repaying his employer's kindness by stealing from him.

Biting the hand that feeds you is the expression that comes to mind, and in this case, biting it extremely hard.

However, although my grandfather may not have been cut out for his tailoring work, surely stealing wasn't the answer either.

A pity his boss didn't have the measure of him in the circumstances.

When he had stolen the rolls of cloth, they would have then been split up and sold onto the black market and to other various contacts that he would have made in the criminal community.

Word would have got around about my grandfather and his criminal activities and that he had cloth to sell, and so more would have been required to be stolen to order, and sold on, again and again.

My grandfather would have made hundreds of dollars from his crimes, which by today's prices would be the equivalent of many thousands of dollars.

In a subsequent newspaper article reporting the details of a later criminal trial which related to him, it was stated that my grandfather had embezzled $1200 from his employer at this time.

A quick conversion using an online calculator tells us that this would be the equivalent of over $50,000 at today's valuation, and so, it was a major crime spree.

Reading newspaper articles relating to my grandfather when he was at school, it seems he had taken part in a half-mile relay race, and he was also good at the long jump.

As a boy, he had not run fast enough on one occasion and was caught red-handed after thieving. As he had already been placed on probation for some of his previous offences, he should have been for the high jump, but as it was his first offence, perhaps the authorities took this into account when he was sentenced, along with the fact he'd lost his father when he was relatively young.

However, despite the support and lenience shown by authorities, my grandfather threw this back into their faces and returned to his criminal ways.

He would appear to have got a kick out of his wrong-doings – a family trait, perhaps, as the second part of this book will demonstrate many similarities with his very devious daughter Miss Y.

My grandfather had repeatedly offended but it seemed that each time he escaped being detected. So even the court had been taken in and had been tricked by my grandfather.

We have newspaper articles referring to his many and varied nefarious activities and these are just some of the many facts and it is just part of the physical evidence that we have uncovered on my grandfather.

Although he was eventually caught by his employer at the time, it didn't prevent my grandfather continuing to lie, deceive and also receive more stolen goods.

The question is: why did he really carry out the crimes in the first place?

Maybe it was falling into and associating with the wrong crowd, or possibly because his family were not financially well off at the time, he had felt he was helping out this way. But it was not the right way to help, of course.

The rest of his siblings had worked very hard to achieve better lives for themselves and had done well. It is highly unlikely they would have agreed with his actions.

Newspaper articles at the time recorded a further incident when my grandfather had appeared in court after pretending to be a Harvard student, charged with being a ticket tout for the annual football game between Yale and Harvard.

A Yale student had paid my grandfather's fine, showed him the sights of New York and then put him up for the night in his own quarters, but the next morning his guest had disappeared with some jewellery and clothes worth around $100.

He was initially arrested by the police but they had to let him go in view of the lack of evidence against him.

The prosecutor began his own investigation and when he learned from a girl of the location that my grandfather had been staying at, he jumped on a train, had my grandfather arrested and he was subsequently brought up before the court.

The magistrate held him on $1,000 bail.

Word went around Harvard that he was not a student there and indeed, the police could find no record of him.

The $100 that was stolen in that incident amounts to $3,084.23 in today's money which is not an insubstantial amount.

My grandfather was given a 12-month jail sentence for his crimes against the Yale students and like the Titanic, my grandfather also went down in 1912, which meant that he should have been released from jail towards the end of 1913. However, it is likely that he was released early having served a much shorter sentence perhaps for good behaviour as we have discovered that he had by then moved from Boston to live with one of his brothers in Maine.

Maybe this was a bail condition in order to ensure that a close eye was kept on him?

However, it then seems that he was soon up to his old tricks again according to a report in *The Boston Globe* in 1913 to the effect that a police officer from the Boston Police Department arrested my grandfather as he was wanted on a charge of larceny.

He was then taken to Dedham in Massachusetts to await trial on the basis of a superior court warrant that had been issued for his arrest.

However, after this my grandfather appears to have no further mention in the newspapers regarding the results of this later trial in Dedham or perhaps he went under an alias?

The question is, was my grandfather then sent to prison again or did he escape and go on the run?

If the latter happened, which now appears to be the case, then it is a bit of a mystery as to how he managed to travel to England which is where he was to turn up next.

Rumours had been passed on down through my grandfather's family and later generations that, at that time, he had gone missing, and had simply disappeared into thin air.

It was reported in newspaper articles many years later that the family had sought help at some point in attempting to locate my grandfather by hiring a Private Investigator as well as placing an advertisement in various issues of local newspapers, in desperate measures to try to track him down, but of course their efforts came to no avail as my grandfather had no intention of being found.

We can't think why he couldn't be found, bearing in mind that we know that less than three years later, one of his family members had definitely been aware of his location and had seemed to be covering for him so as to protect him.

However, that was before his name changed and then continued repeatedly changing, so that his relatives must have eventually finally lost complete contact with him.

Although this aspect of the story was reported directly to us via one of his American descendants, it was added that current day family still did not know what had happened to him, which is perhaps not surprising.

We have since found various newspaper articles dated many years later, starting around 20 years after his initial disappearance, when there was an application to the courts in connection with the administration of the estate of a deceased sibling.

It appears that my grandfather had been a beneficiary under the terms of the Will and the family had little option but to apply to the court to have my grandfather declared dead as he had not been heard from for more than 20 years.

They did advise the court that all attempts to locate him had failed and as a result, they genuinely believed him to be dead.

However, as will be seen later, unknown to his family, my grandfather was by that time married with three children and living on the other side of the world!

It would seem that this court application failed because in 1950 the family made a further approach to the court to have my grandfather declared dead so that the deceased sibling's estate could then be finalised.

If they had known that their youngest brother was still alive but living in another continent, but then how could they have done? If only he could have been made aware that a legacy awaited him back in the USA, no doubt he would somehow have tried to make his way back home!

He only had himself to blame of course for running away from his family in the first place and permanently detaching himself from them.

It was not surprising that my grandfather was believed to have been deceased, as he himself was the one who had continued changing his identity by personal choice.

My grandfather has always been slipping through various nets and that appears to be the way that life was for him, he must have always been glancing over his shoulder in those circumstances.

As the book moves on, it will be seen that there are some passenger lists that have been located and although not relating to his disappearance, maybe there was some other form of transport to escape America that had been used by my grandfather.

This is the most likely option as he must have travelled by some means to reach England, but as yet the method used has not yet been identified and so remains a bit of a mystery.

CHAPTER 3

RUNNING AWAY FROM AMERICA

In 1915, approximately 18 months after his family had last seen him in America, my grandfather reappears but this time, he is in England (as opposed to New England) and is now describing himself as having been born in Canada and therefore representing himself as a citizen of the British Empire.

My grandfather would not have required a passport or a visa to enter Canada from America as there was a cross-border agreement between the two countries, so he was more than likely escaping or disappearing from the police and his larceny charges, crossing the Canadian border to lie low in order to avoid the American authorities, who would have been searching for him.

In addition, passports in the UK did not become mandatory until 1915, so it was likely that he would have been able to enter the country with minimal formalities.

He would have scraped together a living. It was unlikely to have been an honest one, but his 'income' would have needed to be supplemented through any work he could get whilst he built up a plausible false identity, ready for future use with new employers.

It was clear to my grandfather that the Canadian authorities had been keeping a very close eye on him as well, and so it seemed a good time to disappear yet again...?

My grandfather hadn't a clue where he would head off to next, so long as the law could not locate him and return him to the USA to answer the charges that he would no doubt still have to face.

It seems he had at some point developed an affection for horses and racing stables. There had been a rumour from Miss Y, his daughter, that at some stage in his life he had bought and sold racehorses from Argentina to customers in England, Ireland and India.

Whether this was the truth we may never know, as so much of what she said could not ever be relied upon.

Maybe it was a personal preference of my grandfather to rake up manure in the stables, as much as he would have enjoyed raking in the cash from a continuation of the illegal activities that he would have been undertaking in whatever location he was visiting at the time.

My grandfather had become very much a mystery man having simply vanished and then popping up yet again like the bad penny that he was proving to be turning into.

He had then of course continued with his many lies and deceptions as he had just kept repeatedly lying and deceiving in different circumstances, different places and of course in different locations with what appears to be absolutely no remorse whatsoever.

It always seemed that he had enough money to get about, as well as any necessary travel documents. Additionally, by now, my grandfather would have had a collection of several forged papers that he had been collecting in the various places over time.

Reference was made earlier to my grandfather entering Canada, and then subsequently travelling to the UK. He appears to have made a sufficiently believable claim of Canadian identity which was blatantly untrue as he was an American by birth.

However, this was sufficiently authentic enough in the eyes of the UK authorities for my grandfather to be accepted by the British military and this had then allowed him to be enlisted and treated as British and to serve in the Armed Forces as a citizen of the Commonwealth, under yet another new alias.

Perhaps by now my grandfather had an accomplice on his travels who was able to assist him?

Evidence of his travel both to and from Canada has so far proven to be elusive despite his false entry to the Army as a Canadian.

However, he must have travelled from somewhere, bearing in mind the criminal activities and the prison terms that he had been sentenced to whilst he was still living in America. He would have needed to get out of America and change his name so as to enlist in the Army and turn his back on his old life by covering it up and burying it, or so he had thought!

However at present, the specific passenger lists or evidence of whichever form of travel he had used have not yet been located.

My grandfather undertook quite a bit of travelling, to and from different countries around the world, always as a passenger on a steam ship, no doubt aided and abetted by calling in favours from the contacts he had made during his many travels.

At some point, my grandfather had turned up in parts of Wales, and also in Ireland. As with most of his visits, these trips seemed to be mere short-term stopovers.

My grandfather seems to have paid a very high price for his lifestyle, by not being with his family, and not seeing much of his own children either as they were growing up, but no doubt his lifestyle remunerated him well in return for these forfeits.

My grandfather had moved around quite a bit travelling under many different circumstances sometimes in a military capacity and sometimes as a civilian, but once again under yet more new names!

In more up-to-date times, family myths only refer to him by the latest name – just one of his many false identities.

However, slowly but surely the truth has indeed been extracted from many of his various locations, unearthing a large amount of information that we know is accurate as opposed to the fiction and lies supplied by one of the remaining current day family of my grandfather, as in his daughter Miss Y.

For me, his granddaughter, this has proved to be a fruitful and worthwhile research exercise and quite a learning curve.

It has taken several decades to uncover the true facts as so much of the information that was offered by his family in England was untrue.

The information that had been far from simple to discover or unravel was eventually established as a result of the various errors, omissions and mistakes made by my grandfather only for them to be repeated at a much later time once again by Miss

Y his daughter, although in different time periods and in different circumstances.

This still had formed the basis for the research that in time, would prove beyond all reasonable doubt that this father and daughter double act were a thoroughly rotten pair at times and sometimes appear to be inhuman beings in addition to this 'deja vue' feeling that is evident here.

Both these characters, my grandfather and Miss Y have failed miserably to succeed in covering up their tracks either sufficiently or successfully and whilst this has proved to be just plain and simply shoddy and exceptionally inadequate in the circumstances, it was also extremely useful and helpful for anybody that may be looking to validate any information on either of them.

In addition to the inaccurate information, deviousness and the cover-ups, rumours and lies that have been handed down from generation to generation in England as being accurate and factual, have proved to have been purely and simply just made up.

In any case, stories have been passed down the generations such that the waters have been thoroughly muddied with regards to my infamous grandfather. What have now become something of family myths have made my grandfather look a completely different character to the person that he really had been. He had not only lied to and deceived the authorities as well as members of the public, but also, much more importantly, those who were much closer to him at home. One wouldn't think that so many lies and deceptions could be carried out by just one single person but unfortunately, they have been.

As well as having changed his name several times, my grandfather had passports in his various names, including in the surname that his family in England knew him by, but not ever in his original birth surname as he hadn't needed a passport during the time period following his departure from America.

It has already been mentioned that one of his family back in his hometown appeared at first to have stayed loyal to him and kept schtum regarding his whereabouts. It would have been the natural thing to do to protect a younger sibling, but there is only so much that can be done in the circumstances of my grandfather.

His family and widowed mother must have wondered what could have happened to him and where he had disappeared to, but my grandfather had made it into an impossible task to unravel.

Although he had tried to cover his tracks, there is only so much you can conceal, as after all he has been discovered by us.

Perhaps my grandfather had felt twinges of guilt and had regrets, but I think this is unlikely.

All the evidence of my grandfather and his activities that we have, is being kept private and our family tree is strictly offline which is where it will continue to stay as it has been thirty years of hard work and of unravelling by ourselves.

CHAPTER 4
ARMY RECORDS

We discovered a record that at the time we did not realise how vitally important it was going to turn out to be much later in our research. At the time of this initial discovery, it was just one single page that had at that stage been made available to the public but what turned out to be a 20-page document when the whole record was released after expiry of it's private and confidential status.

This document is a military service record that we had fortunately saved originally and when we discovered that the whole document was available from the Ministry of Defence, it was downloaded.

We were simply blown away at the content as it proved beyond any doubt that the soldier referred to was indeed my grandfather. Crucially, after more diligent research, the link between him and his family in Boston was clear to see, as was evidence that one of his sisters would have known of his whereabouts.

What had also clinched it, was that there was a reference to the correct first names of each of his parents, although these were shown on the military record with the false surname that he had also later used on his marriage certificate.

By cross-referencing these names to the American census and also the directories of the city where his parents were supposedly living, we found their real surname at the time of the family immigration from Eastern Europe.

This military record also showed the married name of a family member who was shown as his next of kin at the time.

Initially, the Army had tried contacting his mother. However, she had not replied from her last known address as the letter had been addressed to one of his fake surnames, so it was returned by the Postal Service as not known at the address.

My grandfather had then given the Army a name and address of one of his married sisters as a next point of contact and next of kin.

This has been recorded on his Army records and is a matter of official fact.

Once again, by checking the marriage records for the American state concerned along with the city directories, we were able to trace further details of the person concerned and this information then helped to confirm that they were definitely one and the same family.

Little did my grandfather realise but it was also one of the major factors in helping us to confirm his actual identity and his ancestral origins, along with what my DNA test results showed, proving my connection.

The document has been scanned and is now securely archived by us with a substantial quantity of other family history related documents.

Our archives consist of many boxes of very, very interesting family history records, some paper but many more scanned, backed up and saved in the cloud.

Also archived are numerous, photographs, newspaper cuttings and articles, all of which have been essential to our research.

We have mentioned that in the UK, passports were not compulsory for travel until 1915, and so of course until that point, my grandfather could have travelled to most places worldwide, although Europe would require some proof of identity.

We have also mentioned that he managed to cross the border into Canada and then to join the British Army under the alias of being Canadian and therefore a member of the British Empire.

It must be borne in mind, though, that England was heavily involved with the conflict of World War One at the time, and if someone showed up on the Army's doorstep asking to sign up to serve King George, it is unlikely there would have been many questions asked at a time when military conscription had not commenced.

When serving in a military capacity, travel was of course provided and so no outlay was required, although records had been provided as evidence of his departure places and destinations for my grandfather. Whether these records are complete given his name changes we cannot know. Probably not.

Whilst he was in the military, the posting that my grandfather was given had added to his knowledge of and experience with horses, and the horsemanship that would be a feature later in his personal life.

One of the brothers in law of Miss Y had certainly kept and ridden horses and this has been proven and also witnessed by me, so could this have been the reason for the embellishment of the truth? After all, seeing is believing, right?

To act as a cover-up, my grandfather would always be deceitful even when completing official military records and in different parts of the world, at different times and dates.

It must have been exceptionally difficult for his direct family, not knowing what could have happened to him. I imagine they feared the worst.

It's not surprising though that his siblings had effectively written him off and believed him to have been dead, more like dead wood in the roots of his family tree.

His name and identity had been slowly diluted and it would have seemed extremely strange to his mother if she had been aware of him continually changing his original identity. Also, this would have been upsetting from his mother's viewpoint, as his surname was part of his Jewish roots. Plus, he married outside of his faith.

It appears that he hadn't wanted to be found or discovered and perhaps he had felt ashamed of his somewhat shady past and so deliberately disguised this not ever expecting to be found out.

Although a family member had attempted to remain in contact with my grandfather, unfortunately anything that may have been known had been taken to their grave, so far as we are aware – but from everything we do know, it would seem he had permanently detached himself from his American life as well as his siblings.

Either of my grandparents, possibly both, had exaggerated to the family that he had served as a high-ranking senior officer in the forces, when in fact he had only received a mere temporary commission at a much lower rank as a reserve in the Indian Army, having been transferred from his original British Army post in 1918.

The myth was then of course passed down through the generations as fact.

A further example of my grandfather's deceit was that he had an existing hernia injury which had been recorded originally on his military application form which had been completed following his medical examination when he applied to join the army. However, he then claimed this to be a new injury which had occurred during military training, whilst riding on his horse at the time.

The injury was therefore noted as having happened during active service in the forces and subsequently he had received military hospital treatment and supposedly, a sum of money would also have been received as compensation for the alleged injury.

The Officer who investigated this alleged incident and supported the allegations in a formal report was likely later reprimanded for it.

Perhaps he was a partner in that crime or an accomplice and received a share of the proceeds for his silence?

The lives of my grandfather's siblings, and in turn their families, are such that they would appear to have done reasonably well for themselves, along with their children and grandchildren. They all appear to have stayed out of trouble and out of the newspapers.

I have to say that I feel somewhat cheated that I knew nothing of my American relatives until all of this information came to light. I would have liked to have known the relatives who were left behind as well as their descendants.

In the 1920 American census, after my grandfather had moved on, some members of his family, including his mother, still lived in Boston.

It seems he was the 'bad apple' of the family, and that this trait in him was passed on to one of his daughters, Miss Y, who is discussed in Part Two of this book.

My maternal grandmother had been born and raised in India by her Irish father who was in the British Army and who had been posted overseas. Her mother was described as Eurasian.

This means that my maternal grandmother would have had a European grandfather (this is confirmed as he was Irish) and an Asian grandmother.

My maternal grandmother's family had consisted of her parents, and 4 siblings.

My maternal great-great-grandmother would have been Indian but it is highly likely that her name had been changed to an anglicised version, as was the procedure then.

This seems a shame as our ancestry is fact, so why try to change it? It makes the ancestral lineage sometimes quite difficult to uncover, as it would have proven to be of a pure Indian descent on part of that side of the family.

One of my maternal grandmother's siblings had unfortunately died at a young age.

Another sister of my maternal grandmother married a somewhat younger gentleman but much later in life when compared to my grandparents, as she was over 40 years of age at the time of her wedding. Her husband was a merchant seaman by occupation.

Having been told two separate stories by two of my maternal grandparents' children, one being that one of my maternal grandmother's siblings had married quite young to an older man whereas the other sibling had said that she had married later in life to a younger man but either way, my maternal grandmother had supposedly fallen out with her sister as she hadn't had children which is a bit of a harsh attitude!

We do of course have the birth, marriage and death certificates of two of my maternal grandmother's siblings.

A great uncle through my maternal grandmother's line was believed to have been an accountant by profession and had also married in Ireland, having by then moved overseas from India and he had continued to live there until he himself had passed away in the 1980s.

The couple had produced children but as they are likely to still be alive, the information that we have obtained will remain confidential to protect their privacy.

All the information above was discovered during a trip we made to Ireland for family history purposes to enable us to order and collect certificates, photograph houses and graves as well as locating various other bits of information there too.

It was rumoured to be true but isn't necessarily factual, that my maternal grandmother had fallen out with some of her siblings and saw very little of them throughout her lifetime.

CHAPTER 5
POST ARMY
UP TO 1933

After the end of his military service, my maternal grandfather had initially worked in a civilian sales capacity overseas before he met the woman who was to eventually become his future wife, my grandmother.

It is not known what the commodities were that he was selling or whether he was employed or ran his own business on a self-employed basis.

On the face of it they were very different, culturally and by their nationalities, with my grandfather having been born in America and my future grandmother having been born in India.

Both had very strong but opposing religious beliefs, my grandfather being Jewish and his future wife, a staunch Catholic.

My grandfather's criminal past in America is very unlikely to have been made known to his future wife, who had no similar record.

But, they must have enjoyed each other's company, and were clearly attracted to one another as my future grandmother had become pregnant before they were married unless it was a case of deception by conception.

Did my grandfather trap himself a wife to look good in the public eye: a churchgoing, hard-working, family man?

The true facts on the marriage of my maternal grandparents are that it had started off very much on the wrong footing, with lies.

We have the full marriage details but from a London archive and not from an online source.

My grandmother would possibly have been aware of my grandfather's religion when they met, but definitely so when they eventually married.

As my grandmother was very strong in her own religious beliefs as a Catholic, could this have been a contributory factor towards their eventual marriage break-up less than a decade later?

This is possible, but unlikely.

However, the religious differences between my grandparents may have played no part whatsoever in their marital problems and perhaps it was true love, at least in the beginning, even if it was not an everlasting relationship.

The reason for their marriage break-up and for them to eventually be living so far apart on a permanent basis is almost certainly because he was working hard for his family but from quite some distance away from them.

Ultimately, only the couple themselves truly know why they split.

It was alleged that there was the birth of a first child just a few months after the marriage ceremony, based on a birth date later provided on an official document by that child, but we now know and have proved that both the birth date and year provided were incorrect.

More recently, some new legal information has come to light which states that this first child was born earlier than was originally stated by the family and this means that previous information, including any photographs of him that have been provided are lies.

Even an old photograph with a handwritten note on the back of it, mentioning the wrong year, possibly to conceal the truth. The saying that every picture tells a story is just a tad off course and my grandfather might or might not have been the father of this first child.

Secrets and cover-ups were and still are, it appears, part of the norm with most of this family.

Having made contact directly with the authorities for the church where the next two siblings were baptised, it has been confirmed that the first child, a boy, had not been baptised in the same church as his siblings, and this is now confirmed as the authorities searched for two years either side of the alleged birth year to no avail.

We have some other information that we obtained on the education of this first child. Sadly though he will always be merely a face in a photograph, along with some very limited school records, due to him having passed away, as a young adult, well before my birth.

Maybe my grandfather was merely appearing to be chivalrous by marrying my grandmother, and was doing the right thing by her. Who knows?

We have now obtained the first child's death certificate along with other documentation which provides some revealing facts such as the real place and cause of his sudden death, different to the myth perpetuated by the family.

Obviously, my grandmother would have known the truth, but whether my grandfather did is not certain.

A birth certificate only has the name of the parents based on the information provided at the time by the informant on it.

Anything that anyone in the family has said could be fact or fiction.

The marriage date of my maternal grandparents is a confirmed fact. We have physical proof of that by way of their full marriage certificate, but once again there is deception here.

When my grandparents did marry, the certificate shows my grandfather under yet another false name.

As his father had already been deceased for 15 years prior to the date that the marriage had taken place, and as his mother, still alive had continued to live in America, she would have been unaware of his marriage, as would his remaining American family members.

The full marriage certificate of my grandparents did show the correct Christian names of his parents, and this was a major error on the part of my grandfather which gave us sufficient additional evidence to enable us to track back on various family historical facts. We spent many research hours trying to locate his birth in the USA under this false name. It was only that military record that we referred to earlier along with other information that we already had that eventually enabled us to track down and confirm his original family members.

We are presuming that one of the reasons for the marriage taking place overseas had been that he was marrying outside of his Jewish religion, in addition to his criminal past.

It now appears that my grandfather had continued to practise his Judaism, so showing some honesty here at least.

Perhaps when he had married it had been true love for them, and settling down had changed him, but who knows for certain.

Eventually, he separated from his wife, but rumours from Miss Y who said that they had divorced, although no confirmation of this has been found.

We do have my maternal grandmother's death certificate which confirmed her married name but suggestions of a divorce are only based on information provided by the person registering the death and must not be taken as the gospel truth. A photograph we have shows my grandfather around 1948 wearing his original wedding ring, so any divorce is extremely unlikely to have occurred prior to then.

When my grandfather visited England on his frequent trips, he is rumoured to have mingled with the Jewish community and had Jewish friends, so he was still a practising Jew whilst in England too – something that had held good on his roots from childhood.

Any current living family members from England apart from myself, produced pure fiction to seemingly cover up, the truth.

The true facts have now been laid bare and have slowly been uncovered from various sources through official government, legal and church documentation from many places in different countries.

Further information and facts will continue to be located as a genealogist's job is never complete and we will make further progress along the long, long road of deception. We will find out.

In summary, my maternal grandparents had lived together as a married couple in India, for almost 10 years and during this time, they produced three children with the mystery first child no longer remaining a mystery as his death certificate tallies with what we now know to be the correct birth year. But we do not know why his parents, would have married in Bombay and then not have this child baptised in the same city? Instead, the baptism took place over 80 miles away from the family home. Possibly to reduce embarrassment over having a child born out of wedlock, perhaps?

We do have some photographs of the first child that were taken in India when he was a young boy but unfortunately, there is a gap in the evidence as there were no further photographs made available until he was in uniform in World War Two. We now have a vast amount of information by way of paperwork and certification. It is certainly not fiction but the result of thirty years of diligent research. It may be a long time but we plan on continuing, as the more we uncover the more we will know the truth.

CHAPTER 6
MARRIAGE
SEPARATION

The cracks in the marriage of my maternal grandparents appeared less than 10 years after their marriage nuptials had taken place, and in addition, it also appears that their final separation occurred less than 12 months after Miss Y's birth.

It is a possibility that the birth of Miss Y could have been a contributory factor towards my grandparents eventually splitting up and for my grandmother then to move over 4,500 miles away from my grandfather.

Apart from this, it would have been a huge step to have taken with both the distance and the separation making things quite impossible for my grandparents to have had much contact or of course for their children to be within proximity of their father, so presumably there must have been a huge error, misunderstanding or deceit on one or both of their parts.

There must surely have been major reasons, but whatever those reasons were, they will remain a secret. It had been suggested by one family member that my grandmother had engaged in an affair and as a result of this alleged liaison, that my grandfather may not have necessarily been the father of Miss Y. Whilst not conclusive, very early photographs of Miss Y show her with a substantially different appearance to her siblings in terms of complexion and hair style.

Miss Y's version was that it was my grandfather who she had believed to have had an affair and that this was the reason that my maternal grandmother had left India to start a new life in England, but this was of course purely speculation on the part of Miss Y.

My grandfather has however since been proven to be the father of Miss Y and this has been scientifically proven, following the DNA test that I took. My father also did DNA testing and by separating his genes, there is a clear path back to my maternal grandfather, thus proving his origins.

I have now discovered that I share several significant genetic markers with current-day descendants of my grandfather and his siblings.

The test also confirms the Jewish bloodline, albeit only just over 25% for myself due to my grandmother not being of Jewish origins.

Miss Y was just 7 months old when she and her family first left India in the early 1930s but had then returned to their home in the Malabar area of Bombay four months later, on a short-term basis with my maternal grandmother destined to move her family to England permanently a short while later.

During that first trip to England, my grandmother appeared to be looking at possible residential properties, as we now know that she was preparing for an impending separation and move overseas just a few months later.

These journeys would definitely have been arduous trips to make with young children, but there are official passenger list records from the Board of Trade in the UK showing my maternal grandmother travelling both from India to England, the return trip to Asia and the final leg to England, accompanied by the children on each occasion.

My grandfather did look after his wife and his family and kept them well financed, but this would have been the expectation as this was a requirement of his faith to put his wife first.

They were obviously on a long-term separation for whatever the reasons had been, but this eventually became a permanent arrangement.

It seems exceptionally odd though that whilst my maternal grandmother was born and had spent her entire life in India, including getting married there, she had then moved overseas to the UK, despite this being a place that she appears to have only ever visited before on the two trips mentioned above, as can be evidenced from official Government paperwork.

So, she had then moved away from India effectively on a permanent basis, and not only was it a very long distance from my grandfather at some 4,500 miles, but also at the relatively young age of 33 years old and much too far away distance wise for the children to have seen their father whilst growing up.

Without knowing the area or ever having travelled there previously, my maternal grandmother had just seemingly moved to England on a permanent basis after her second journey, taking with her the then two youngest children and an ayah who was an Indian national and was included on the passenger list and employed as a maid and nanny.

My grandmother and her children, along with the ayah, subsequently lived together as a family unit in rented houses in many different areas of the country.

Some of these homes were in various places within the boundaries of London, Jersey in the Channel Islands, two houses in Surrey, one in Farnham and one in Kingston upon Thames as well as several properties in the Sussex region. At no time, however, did they return to their original birth place in India.

Following this, did my maternal grandparents have something to hide, as over the next 15 years my grandmother and the children lived at a minimum of 10 different addresses?

The family always appear to be on the move, not staying in one place too long but just kept moving around time and again, from place to place, but why?

The ship that my maternal grandmother had travelled on was the P&O RMS Viceroy of India. This was a steam ship and the family would have enjoyed complete luxury as would be expected from first class travel.

As an example, the passenger facilities on board the ship included an indoor salt-water swimming pool and was more than just a comfortable way to travel at the time.

A sign of the times and how Indian-born natives were treated in the era of British rule in India prior to the 1947 partition was that the ayah, who was a servant, with her main responsibility being to look after the children, did not have a cabin, but instead travelled in 3rd class which was a sleeping area on the open deck!

Because the original nationality of my maternal grandfather was American, my grandmother automatically became American once they were married, and so she was recorded as an alien on immigration records following her arrival into England after their first voyage. As a result of this, she was required as a condition of her visa to report to Bow Street police station in London every week for her papers to be inspected so that she would be permitted to stay in the UK for an extended period.

According to the UK Government Home Office citizenship records, my grandfather became naturalised as a British citizen in 1933 and as a result, because of the nationality rules, my maternal grandmother herself then also automatically became a British subject and no longer had to undergo her weekly visits to the police station.

However, as my maternal grandfather was already falsely declaring to be British by virtue of him having described himself as having been born in the commonwealth country of Canada, a place which he himself had written down and had supplied as one of his many false multiple birthplaces, why would my grandfather feel it was necessary to naturalise yet again? Why wasn't this act of deceit discovered at the time of his naturalisation application, by comparing the information shown on the application against the facts shown in his military records?

How times appear to have changed in modern times in terms of people having to provide multi factor authentication of their identities just to open a bank account, take out an insurance policy or even make an online purchase. Compare this with the early days of my grandfather whilst undertaking his illegal travels using his many and various identities.

Well, those are the questions that we would like to know the answers to but may never discover!

We have obtained a copy of his official Government-issued naturalisation certificate and this contains some useful background information, confirming the alias that he was using at the time was still the same as when he had married, 10 years earlier.

Although subject to file closure rules, some years ago we applied to the Home Office of the British Government for copies of the full naturalisation application file for my grandfather.

We were told that these files would have contained a substantial amount of detailed background information, but the response was the disappointing news that the file had already been destroyed, even though there were still 12 years to go before its correct closure date of 75 years.

The reason given was that they didn't have enough space to store them all, but this lacks credibility and legality as the documents would still have been subject to the closure rules and so should have been retained for the full 75 years before being disposed of.

What secrets would those files have contained, if any?

After settling in the UK, my maternal grandmother had subsequently managed to make some friends of her own, as well as enjoying a more intimate relationship, sufficiently so that she would again get herself in the family way, resulting in the birth of two additional children in 1939.

Despite it being 6 years following the marital and geographical separation of my maternal grandparents, my grandfather was stated as being the father of these two children on their official birth certificates. However, information on a certificate is only based on what an informant states to the Registrar.

Although it is unlikely, my grandfather could have been the father, as although he was by all accounts several thousand miles away, could he have visited his family and had relations with my grandmother some 9 months before the births?

This needed checking but my grandfather does not appear on any passenger lists during the time between the departure of my grandmother in 1933 and the likely conception date of the two children in 1939.

The rest of the current family prefer to believe that he was unlikely to have been the father but he could have used another false name for his travelling. It is possible. He has form! We do have a photograph that suggests that he could have travelled from India as the couple in the picture are my grandparents and they are sitting together in the garden of a property with architectural features that look to be very English.

They had certainly both looked older than the ages that they would have been at the time that they had departed India and could have been in the same vicinity at the same time as the photograph appeared to depict.

Having shown the photograph in question to another relative and her husband without giving any clues as to the possible time period or their ages, they were of the same opinion that my maternal grandparents were at least 10, probably 15 years older in the garden photograph than the snapshot that had been taken in India before my grandmother had left India prior to her 1933 departure date.

However, the two extra children were born prior to World War Two starting in September 1939 and this was only 6 years after my grandmother had left India and that was when international leisure travel would not have been possible.

Unfortunately, none of the children were actually in the photograph, as it may otherwise have been easier to date it.

If, however, we consider that the first voyage by my grandfather that we located in the records was in 1948, this would have been exactly 15 years later and therefore, an equally likely date.

This would therefore suggest that the two later children who were born outside of India were unlikely to have been my grandfather's children, but it is not beyond the realms of impossibility as it must be borne in mind that my grandfather's name appeared on their birth certificates.

Neither of my grandparents ever remarried, to the best of my knowledge, but there were various rumours as to another candidate who might be the father of the two later additions to the family. Miss Y and her siblings suggested that the father was a drunken Irishman who was said to be more than an occasional visitor to the family home.

The evidence discovered and verified to date points in the direction of an itinerant Irishman by the surname of Flynn.

Perhaps he really was just a male friend and nothing more than that. However, most of the current day family are, as per usual, presuming it to be true without knowing the real facts or examining any evidence that there might be.

As it is, my maternal grandmother is the only one who knows the truth.

The Irishman, Flynn had three forenames and we were also given a birth date for him by one of the additional two children. However, we located "our" Flynn in the official birth records and he had the same birth date but a birth year with an 8-year difference to the one given. Both Flynns were born in the same city.

What proved to be really interesting though, was the discovery of several newspaper articles that reported the arrest of an Irishman with the exact same name as the man in question, stating that he had subsequently appeared in court charged with defrauding various ladies in the town of Worthing where my grandmother was living at the same time.

Mr Flynn was falsely claiming to have been a wealthy man, temporarily down on his luck and 'borrowing' relatively large sums of money from his female victims.

The reason that we have matched this man as the alternate father is that the court records mention a specific physical defect (which will remain private) – there is no doubt that this was one and the same man. Miss Y and her siblings in their anecdotes describe the Irishman who was the visitor to their home as having the exact same physical defect.

He was alleged to have made my grandmother pregnant with the result being the two later children. But, as we said earlier, paternity equally could have been my grandfather's responsibility.

Only a DNA test performed by each of the children while they were still alive could have confirmed it.

My maternal grandmother gave birth to each of her children in places where birth certificates were not so easy to come by, unlike England where we have the General Register Office which is so convenient and easy to access.

It seems that my maternal grandmother was attracted to criminal characteristics in her partners: my grandfather, and this Irish friend, Flynn.

One of the mysteries surrounding my grandmother and her new-found life as a British resident is how was her lifestyle funded and by whom?

It would seem to be that the family presumed it to be my grandfather as based on the newspaper articles, Flynn was more practised at taking money off ladies in his life than financing them.

Perhaps several men were able to help contribute towards the financial aspect of her and the children? Maybe she was in receipt of separate additional funding directly from or on behalf of my grandfather whilst he was working overseas in India.

As mentioned earlier, it is unclear why my grandmother would choose to go to England in the first place? We have managed to confirm that she had only once set foot on British soil before her move to England. That was shortly after her marriage when her name was on a passenger list returning to India after a trip to Ireland with her mother and sister. She had no prior knowledge of the various areas that they had lived in. One of her brothers may have been an influence, as he had moved from India and was living in Ireland, but then if this was the case, why would she choose England rather than Ireland?

The eldest child was already attending a private school in England, so perhaps that had been the reason for needing to have an English residence. Still, it meant a very long distance between husband and wife meaning that the family would have rarely seen or heard from my grandfather, although he stayed for around six months at a time on his trips to England as he almost certainly would have disliked the onset of the monsoon season in the south western part of India. The severity of the adverse weather where he had made his home would have been most unpleasant.

The journeys for my grandfather that have been verified from official records took place over a 7-year time period.

Each of these trips were to England from India and the return legs, so why was there such a huge gap of 15 years between my grandmother moving to England in 1933, before my grandfather came to this country for business purposes but also to visit his family?

Even bearing in mind that the Second World War was taking place between 1939 and 1945, there are still two quite substantial gaps between 1933 and 1939 and then from 1946 to 1947 when my grandfather would presumably have had quite a few opportunities to visit his family.

Perhaps the travelling had not been viable financially or for some other reasons.

The period that he had travelled and lived in England for temporary periods dated from the spring of 1948 through until quite late in 1954. These are proven facts and so there appears to be on the surface, a huge gap in years that is currently unexplained between when the family came over to England in 1933 that has so far not been accounted for.

Perhaps my grandfather reinvented himself with another alias, and then he would have been able to visit and stay freely to see his family members without his known details being recorded on passenger lists.

What a complicated web was woven here.

Miss Y has stated that she had never seen any evidence to enable her to form a proper opinion of my grandfather as she had supposedly only met him on two of the occasions that he came over from India but then that suited Miss Y to be left to her own devices as will be explained later in this book.

It seems that my grandfather had perhaps been up to his old and dirty tricks.

He was recorded on passenger lists and also in Indian business records sometimes as a Publisher and on other occasions as a Proprietor, but was his occupation part of his disguise and used for covering up, whilst somebody else did the work whilst he collected the rewards?

My grandfather seemed to have changed his name almost as frequently as his underwear, so going by that he could do anything and be anyone at any time.

According to Miss Y, she recalls that she had observed my grandparents kissing in a room at one of her childhood homes, approximately 8 years following the births of her most recent siblings.

It was at this time that Miss Y alleges that my grandfather had invited her to leave England and return to his home in India to live with him on a permanent basis around 1946 or 1947.

However, as there is no passenger list recording him as coming into the country or indeed leaving in this two-year period, this looks to be untrue.

Maybe this was wishful thinking on her part?

Miss Y also alleged that the second occasion on which she had met my grandfather had been on the occasion of her 21st birthday in 1952. It is questionable as to whether this happened, as by that time she had not only moved away from the family residence in Worthing and was then living in Kent, shortly to marry for the first of what would be a number of times.

As a researcher searches and continues to diligently search, then the more the truth and facts will be discovered, untangled but eventually fall into the right place.

We might never know the true facts on whether my grandfather was of good financial standing but if he could tell us, I wonder what he would say?

It would appear he did perhaps change his ways, moving from his early days of crime to earning an honest living, but then he was 4,500 miles away from the rest of his family, so who can be sure...

The eldest child of my grandparents passed away during World War Two. He was killed in a collision with another aircraft whilst flying his hurricane in Scotland, a fact that we have uncovered as a result of viewing his actual death certificate and the Royal Air Force report following the official investigation of the incident.

This contradicted the story given to us by Miss Y that he had died when his aircraft engine had frozen over Carlisle, causing him to crash, despite the location of the accident having been written on the back of a photograph in the handwriting of my grandmother.

We cannot begin to imagine the sense of loss following an incident of this nature. My grandmother is said to have become temporarily paralysed by shock after her first child had died, as it is said that a fortune teller, years before, had predicted to her that this event was going to happen. However, it was Miss Y that told us about the fortune teller story, so maybe true, maybe not.

The funeral of my uncle took place at a cemetery local to where they lived at the time and he was buried in a Commonwealth War Grave. Nobody from the family, apart from ourselves, has ever visited at any point to pay their respects. Even Miss Y by her own admission failed to call at her elder brother's last resting place. She would have been ten years old and probably too young to attend the funeral, but admitted that she did not visit at a later date.

The youngest two children were under 5 years of age when their brother died. It is said that the elder sister of Miss Y took care of the household for approximately a year, while my grandmother grieved, even though she would have been under 15 years of age herself at the time.

Given that Miss Y did not attend the funerals of her mother or her sister and by her own admission has never paid her respects at their graves, she clearly avoids any difficult situation.

By contrast, when it was discovered that my grandmother had been buried along with another child's cremated remains and both of them were in an unmarked grave near Worthing, my husband and I arranged for a headstone to be erected at the cemetery concerned to ensure that their memories were not forgotten.

Knowing where to look and how to go about finding things from our proven experience of research and the pure determination to find out the truth has helped along this long and bumpy road of discovery.

It involved visiting all the right archives, on many occasions in different parts of the country including national centres in London as well as County Record Offices in other provincial areas. We also made contact with family members in India and also America. This proved to be of great importance to uncover documentation and to find the physical proof resulting in a major pile of paperwork that has now been safely organised and filed away.

It was a mammoth task to unravel the tangled web of deception which had clearly continued throughout the life, times and ultimately even following the death of my grandfather.

Identifying and collecting the many different types of documents has resulted in the wearing out of shoe leather, in addition to using many gallons of petrol over a very long time period in order to uncover the truth and the facts about my grandfather one way or another.

It's not often that the words 'truth' and 'my grandfather' appear in the same sentence unfortunately!

But some of the research has also been paid for and investigated by hiring a firm of solicitors in India with the right contacts, but that has proved to be an exceedingly long and very slow and at times expensive process, but worth every penny, as you cannot ever put a price on family.

A lot of the original information on my grandfather had been either made up, exaggerated, or withheld at the time when enquiries were made to family members, despite asking them repeatedly over a long period of time.

The quest for information turned into a worldwide journey of discovery of the many deliberate deceptions and cover-ups.

This had included the actual date of birth and birthplace of my grandfather along with the true identity of his parents as proven on American birth records and on various American censuses. They were correctly recorded as being of Eastern European Jewish descent and not Americans as we had been led to believe from the outset by current relatives, specifically Miss Y.

It was partly our own fault of course for naively believing what we had been told and for accepting it without question. We certainly will not believe any more statements without first finding some confirmed source to evidence what is being said.

If there is one very important lesson that has been learned from all of this and that is never to assume that information is correct until you have evidence proving it.

In the case of other people and their families it may be an assumption that any information that is provided by family members must be true because it has been given by a relative.

However, it is important to bear in mind that sometimes errors, myths, rumours and simply a bad memory can also be a feature of family lore. False information may not always be intentional dishonesty as in our case, but sometimes is given to enhance or protect an ancestor's reputation.

Memories can and frequently do play tricks, and can also fade with time. Sometimes mistakes can be passed down through generations.

Just occasionally though there are deliberate deceptions which occur in order to attempt to cover up the smallest detail or something much bigger.

It is always recommended that a researcher should find at least two legitimate sources to validate a fact, but it is preferable to try to locate a minimum of three written sources as future physical proof.

It is important to clarify the difference between an original document, a scan, and a transcription. A scan may be illegible due to poor handwriting or low-quality image scanning. A transcription is only someone else's interpretation of a record. An original document is always preferable, where possible.

If there is uncertainty as to what qualifies as an official source or how or where to locate it, ask someone who might have the necessary family history experience or knowledge of a particular sector to provide some assistance along the way.

Never, ever take word of mouth as a fact, as we have ourselves discovered in the past more often than not, the information provided can prove totally incorrect.

There are many places to check your resources out at, such as the British Library Oriental and Asian collection, Archives, History Centres and local libraries amongst others. Where possible, go in person to these depositories and observe, check and obtain proper copies of the correct documents.

Military records should give the correct names, unless the subject is similar to my grandfather. As well as providing an address or addresses for the next of kin along with other valuable information, such as medical information (which can include illnesses, scars, marks and possible injuries that have occurred before or during their service in the armed forces), can all help with your research, as well as proving and confirming the identity of an ancestor and that they are who they were believed to be or more importantly, who they said that they were.

Facts are certainly not obtained by copying from other people's online family trees, as many of them are simply incorrect.

Ages do not always tally exactly so be careful there too. Sometimes there can be a person with the same name and of the same age who may appear to fit the required profile, but if it turns out to be just coincidental, then so be it.

Some people seem to think that an entry is more credible just because it appears on an online database but of course this is not necessarily so, as it could be taken from a transcript and not the original. Take the time to check all facts and sources.

For example, with a census entry from any country, many people do not look at the full details as they do not wish to pay, but as a result they may select the wrong person or worse still, miss the right one! Two people with the same name but only an approximate age and/or birth year could cause confusion, especially if that information is taken forward incorrectly and then copied by others. Unfortunately, plagiarism is rife in family history.

The self-satisfaction that can be enjoyed at all levels of research can only be obtained if a researcher has proper and correct proof of all their documents and facts and always in writing as they need to be spot on with accuracy.

Certificates are a must for family history: births, marriages and deaths, for proper verification and also baptism details. Births, marriages and deaths were certificated by law from July 1837.

A DNA test can be part of the final answer in the quest for facts and can also point you in the direction of other documents. It can prove or disprove rumours on whether something is the truth by matching up with further records that already exist in alternative archives. Of course, not all DNA is 100% accurate.

Most of my grandfather's current day family in England had made their choices to believe in what they wanted to, rather than to make the choice or even to entertain the thought of what the true facts may have been.

This is their personal choice to choose what to believe in, with the result that they must presumably believe the lies but the important thing here is that we now know the real facts and the truth, the whole truth and nothing but the truth.

After all, your real heritage and the history that goes with it is what it is and will always remain in the family as it is. This is what gives a family their true and proper identity especially in this case.

Be proud of what and who you are, as it cannot be changed, even with a false identity as my grandfather seemed to be attempting.

My grandfather and Miss Y, his daughter, were at times on an equal level, both doing similar things, but in different decades, both demonstrating a selfish and self-centred attitude towards their victims, both being very devious people.

But although each of them is different with varying degrees of deception, it was almost certainly with the common aim of increasing wealth, possessions or importance.

CHAPTER 7
FINANCIAL

Various rumours have been circulated and perpetuated over the years and through the generations as to the financial status or otherwise of my grandfather.

Was he rich?

Was he poor?

Rich man, poor man, beggar man, thief is the old saying. The jury is still out as to whether he qualified for the first category even if there is no doubt from what we have proven regarding his earlier life, that he certainly qualified for the last three!

Some of the passenger lists that have been located show that my grandfather had an account with the Mercantile Bank of India in which he would have been able to deposit funds and enable transactions to be made. Wherever the money had come from, it was presumably squirrelled away and used in whichever country my grandfather happened to be living in at the particular time.

There have been several theories as to just how well off he really was.

The family have always believed and indeed have continued to circulate the myth that my grandfather was a multi-millionaire. But if this was the case, what happened to this alleged fortune?

My grandfather had supposedly paid generous amounts to my grandmother towards the cost of housing, food, private schooling for the children and various other expenses and bills which certainly would have added up substantially over the years. It was also said that he paid each of the children a generous monthly allowance.

The question must be asked, who would have benefited from his estate after his death? At this stage, nobody supposedly knows but some people need to wake up and smell the coffee as it's fresher and probably contains more grounds for truth. If my grandfather had intended that some of his finances should be passed on to his greedy and unrealistic family, then surely, he would have made certain that they inherited at the appropriate time by making a properly documented last Will and Testament. Nothing has been found, and our information is that the family members did not receive an inheritance, or at least that is what they told us, and it is highly unlikely that it will happen now as my grandfather supposedly passed away many years ago and so the need is to open their minds to reality.

My maternal grandparents' children have always questioned as to where his money disappeared to but of course, we only believe in the facts and not the usual myths and rumours.

Also, the death of my grandfather has not yet been located, in India or indeed anywhere else in the world.

We were told that he had supposedly died in India, but despite enquiries through the correct channels and the legal system there, nothing has been found, but then just maybe he had used another alias somewhere.

No last will and testament have yet been located and so the truth is still out there somewhere, if there had been a will made in the first place of course.

There have been many and varied slip-ups from the different people concerned in this web of deceit, spreading their unproven rumour that my grandfather had been exceptionally wealthy.

If some huge fortune had existed and that is indeed a big **IF,** we have huge doubts over its existence in the first place.

But, if there had been any assets left in his estate, where were they and who if anyone were the beneficiaries?

We were given one suggestion, which was provided by the second husband of Miss Y. He was a totally honest person without any question and anything he said, we would take as the truth.

He said that his understanding and that he had been informed to this effect, was that the proprietor of The Ambassador Hotel in Mumbai had been the sole beneficiary of the will of my grandfather.

The problem is that this sort of information can only have been provided by either Miss Y or her older sister, as he had no other contacts that could have known this.

If this was true, then this leads to the question as to why, did he leave his estate to the hotel proprietor?

Perhaps it was simply because he had been a very kind and supportive friend.

It was also mentioned that my grandfather was supposed to have spent his final days as a full-time resident at the Ambassador Hotel, so it is possible he owed money for his hotel bill or perhaps there were other debtors and the hotel proprietor acted in the capacity of an executor and settled the debts on behalf of my grandfather?

We have explored the possibility that there may have been some archive records of the hotel and also its ownership in a bid to answer some of these questions, but this hotel no longer exists.

This is not really surprising, bearing in mind the number of years that have elapsed, and so that avenue of enquiry has drawn a blank.

However, both siblings had each separately stated and continued to state throughout the years that followed that they had no idea as to whether there was any will or who would have been the beneficiaries to any estate and yet, one of them, or possibly my grandmother, must have passed the above information to Miss Y's second husband!

The one possibility that occurs to us is that either my maternal grandmother or the older sibling might have secretly inherited, or maybe even the devious Miss Y, although that is perhaps stretching the imagination a little too far ...or is it?

The fact that my maternal grandparents were possibly divorced by the time of my grandfather's death, leads us to think that the older sibling theory has more merit as she would have been aged around 27 or 28 if my grandfather had died at the time that has been suggested.

But wherever and whenever he died, he could have another family that no-one in the UK was aware of and they may have inherited his wealth.

After all, as my grandfather had been seemingly separated from his wife and also the marital bed for over 20 years at the supposed year of his death, could this be yet another act of deceit?

Tracing a will in India is a complex process, especially if it relates to a British subject who died after the partition in 1947.

Firstly, a death certificate has to be found by the correctly authorised people, and it seems that the records are not in the same well archived and indexed state that we have the good fortune to enjoy in England.

It is therefore impossible for an ordinary citizen to obtain copies of these records.

As my grandfather was a British citizen by the time of his death as a result of his earlier naturalisation, it might be expected that the will had been proved in England but unfortunately, this was not the case.

We engaged a solicitor in India to provide research services. Their brief of engagement from us was to investigate and to try and confirm the date and year of death. Additionally, if there were any records pertaining to the will that could subsequently be located to prove the facts rather than guess at the fiction.

Unfortunately, this research has to date proved inconclusive – but we persevere!

Of course, any assets that my grandfather had accumulated during his lifetime may not have been a result of his own financial acumen or from his own endeavours, but had instead been someone else's money, such as a mysterious backer or an investor designed to make it look genuinely as though my grandfather was a very fortunate and wealthy man in his own right.

Therefore, his debts could even have exceeded his assets.

Unfortunately, for the rest of my grandfather's relatives in England, apart from myself, they had never been interested enough to think about undertaking any proper research or to ask the right questions of the right people to discover or find out the truth about him.

However, they were happy enough to just take and accept any financial benefits coming in their direction, without ever giving anything back in return.

Miss Y has always recounted that her mother and the two older siblings born in India that were officially my grandfather's, at least on official paperwork, had received substantial monetary allowances right up until the date of his death, but of course, no evidence of his death has yet come to light.

What would the frequency of these alleged allowances have been and who or where did the money really come from?

Was it honest money?

Unlikely, but nevertheless a possibility.

In addition to the money, it was also said that during World War Two, generous food parcels had been received at the English home where the family were living in Farnham, Surrey.

Accompanying the food were various copies of the magazines from India that were supposedly published by my grandfather.

However, was it my grandfather who had actually sent the food parcels and magazines or somebody else acting on his behalf in the capacity of an agent?

Was it just my grandfather's name on the publishing magazines as a front whilst he was elsewhere?

What is interesting, though, is that the financial allowances referred to earlier reportedly ceased abruptly, coinciding with the possibility of the death of my grandfather, or not.

Of course, this raises additional questions as to whether any money had ever existed at all and if so, where the finance would have come from as the only thing that is certain is the uncertainty itself!

What would the value of the estate have been and how much might have been received by each of the family members in England, if anything?

Returning to the evidence of the completely reliable second husband of Miss Y, in addition to having been told about the Ambassador Hotel, he also stated that he can clearly remember not only the monthly allowance payments being received by Miss Y, but importantly, he also remembers them ceasing.

He also added that the amount received was actually quite substantial and had been more than the amount he received by way of his annual salary at that time, which was in the last few years of the 1950s.

The only problem we have with this is that their marriage did not take place until two years after the suggested death date of my grandfather and if he had already passed away prior to then, it has to be asked where the continuing payments come from and more importantly from whom?

Could Miss Y have been benefiting from another hidden source of income being disguised as her paternal allowance? Maybe she had a well-paid part time occupation?

The alternative is that my grandfather didn't die at the time that has been suggested. So far, a death registration has not been located in India, England or indeed any other place suggested by any of his known aliases.

Indian newspaper archives have also been searched as it would not be unreasonable to expect the passing of a supposedly prominent businessman to have been mentioned.

If there had been a divorce between my grandparents, the fact that his two daughters were by now adults and he would have learned on his visits to England that my grandmother had given birth to two children possibly fathered by another man, may have been the real reasons that the allowance had been stopped, especially as he may have found out that his name had been placed onto the birth certificates, naming him as the father.

Like any man in the same situation, this was said to have made my grandfather angry however, it was Miss Y who reported this fact and so, going on previous experience, may not have been true. So why did the allowances not cease in 1939, the year the children were born? The explanation may be simply that the war started very shortly after the birth and so my grandfather may not have found that his name had been incorrectly used until several years later.

The instant change in the fortune of my grandmother and the children after the allowance ceased was to have severe consequences on their future lifestyle in the same way that the death of my great grandfather in 1908 had affected my grandfather and his family.

However, it does appear that if my grandparents had divorced at some point between 1948 and the date of his death, which now appears to have been the case, at least on the surface, then my grandmother would not presumably have inherited and his children would by now have been adults in their own right so the fact that they may well have been excluded could be an adequate explanation.

Most of this family seem to have been obsessed by my grandfather and his financial status, particularly Miss Y who says she didn't know why she did not receive a legacy and couldn't understand where his money could possibly have disappeared to.

Nobody else knows or is likely to find out the true facts but was my grandfather as wealthy as he was rumoured to have been or perhaps it was a case of my grandfather minding his own business?

Wealth was something the family wanted to believe, as it enhanced their own public status.

It is quite possible that his publishing business – if it was his business – struggled in post-partition India, as British dominance and governance of the country ceased, resulting in a substantial reduction in the number of both British and colonial customers with many having moved back to the UK. It seems that almost overnight, British influence on day-to-day living disappeared.

Possibly, some evidence that does point towards the family being financially well off was the fact that the children in the care of my grandmother were privately educated, having been sent to a variety of independent Catholic schools in and around the London area and beyond.

Could the private schooling of the children have all been part of a benefits package with my grandfather's job as is the practice nowadays? If not the case, where did the money come from?

Judging from photographs, my grandmother and the children appeared to be reasonably well clothed, but once again there has been no financial proof as to how this could have been afforded.

The amount of money required by my grandmother would have needed to be substantial to fund the rent of some of the residences including one in the Kensington area of London and also Surrey as well as seafront properties on the south coast.

In addition, food and drink would have had to be put on the table, as well as the cost of other household consumables and cleaning. It would be necessary to take all of these costs into account as well as the requirement to fund clothing and private schooling for the five children as well.

Anecdotally, we were also told that the children enjoyed horse riding, tennis, and swimming lessons and these could not have come without substantial expenditure, if this was the truth.

Perhaps my grandmother had some inheritance through her parents and so was able to self-fund? This is however unlikely as her father had died in 1923 and despite the family "myth" that he had owned the advertising rights to the Indian railways, he had actually been employed as a railway cleaner, following his retirement from the army and her mother did not pass away until 1948.

It has to be borne in mind that my grandmother did not work for a living and had come from the background in India where ladies were provided for by their menfolk.

When the family came over from India, it will be recalled that they were accompanied by an ayah and whilst she likely would have been paid an absolute pittance, she would still have lived in the household, thus adding yet another mouth to feed.

Miss Y had suggested that my grandfather must have been very well off to be able to provide the funds required as well as financing his own lifestyle back in India. Speculation but probably not inaccurate.

My grandmother must have had some financial support from person or persons unknown as she had certainly never worked. Flynn the Irishman, it will be recalled, was more likely to remove funds than to provide them.

Just before Miss Y was due to marry for the first time, she had said that during one of the regular trips that my maternal grandfather had made over to London, she had supposedly asked him to help provide some funds for her then future husband for a proposed business venture.

Whether or not it was just plain common sense or not on the part of my grandfather, or simply that the figures didn't stack up, he apparently had refused to get involved financially.

Perhaps the real reason was that by now, my grandfather was running low on his finances and although this was a possibility, it was unlikely as this argument is countered by his expensive lifestyle at the time and evidenced by his frequent first-class trips to and from India. More likely he just did not want to get involved.

It is perhaps the case that this funding could have just been borrowed money or perhaps it was the proceeds of his earlier years of crime.

One additional factor perhaps was that my grandfather was said to have been suffering from a specific type of cancer and was seeking medical attention from a renowned Harley Street physician and as these services do not come cheap, perhaps he was by then more careful what he spent money on.

The suggestion has been passed down by Miss Y that my grandfather had passed away in India, the same country where he had married. There is no evidence to substantiate this, however.

My grandfather was prone to change his name so he is far more likely to have passed away under an alias and in another country.

Our facts are better than the myths perpetuated by many other members of this family.

It has been a major effort to prove what has been discovered so far but at the end of the day, all that is wanted is the truth as opposed to the fiction.

CHAPTER 8
WORK AND CAREER

We have already heard of the early career of my grandfather, of both his honest and his dishonest endeavours, albeit mainly dishonest.

His criminal activities as a thief have previously been documented, as have his military activities after fleeing his home country when he was a young adult American.

Although his army achievements were seemingly somewhat exaggerated, it was his life after he had become a civilian that this chapter examines.

When he married, his occupation was simply shown on the marriage certificate as 'Salesman', but what commodities would he have been selling?

Anecdotal evidence from family members is that he was a buyer and seller of racehorses and allegedly having a close friendship with a leading Irish jockey at the time.

There is no physical proof that the friendship with the jockey existed, however. Also, the rest of the family would not have been old enough to have known about the jockey whilst they were living in India but as it was in England that the friendship was supposed to have developed, it is more questionable as it could only have been from 1948 – 1954 unless my grandfather was again under a different name when travelling.

Certainly, his early time in the army was spent attached to equine units and he would have spent a lot of time in the companionship of horses but that proves absolutely nothing.

Remember the injury that he claimed to have sustained during his military years? Well, that was caused (or was alleged to have been caused) whilst my grandfather was dismounting from a horse!

The story passed down through the generations was that he had made his money as a publisher and the alleged delivery to the family home of copies of the publications that he was responsible for, seems to add fuel to the fire of conspiracy.

The name of my grandfather had been mentioned in several Indian Trade Directories from the mid-1930s to the mid-1950s which described him as the publisher of three publications, based in Bombay.

The question is whether my grandfather was the actual owner of this publishing business or indeed whether he was simply an employee working for somebody else.

An employer would have provided a salary as well as expenses paid to him for travel and accommodation as would be the normal arrangement currently as part of a package deal.

The three publications were diverse to say the least. They were a sports newspaper: 'The Sporting Times of India'; a magazine based on the movie industry: 'The Motion Picture Magazine' which was published in both America and India; with the third title extolling the virtues of the Greater Indian Peninsular Railway (GIPR), but as we have not as yet been able to locate a copy, we are uncertain as to whether this is a railway enthusiasts publication or one describing the history of the railway company and the development of the company's rail network.

My grandfather was also mentioned by name in Freemasonry Directories and we have copies of entries from various journals that confirm his membership of the organisation, but whether he took an active part is unknown.

It is quite possible that the supposed wealth would have been the result of deception, taking out loans or by pulling in some of his favours from his contacts in America, connected with his earlier criminal times, or later times as he was after all 4,500 miles away and well out of sight of any relatives.

My grandfather's career, whether as a business owner or an employee, involved a considerable amount of travelling.

There were stop-off points at different locations en route and these could have been well chosen for strategic reasons. There is little evidence as to what activities he was engaged in whilst away from his home in India.

It is always possible of course that my grandfather had travelled on different routes to other countries under yet more aliases.

At present, we only have records of his travels from India to England followed by the appropriate return journey on various occasions.

So let us examine the journal of my grandfather's journeys.

Certainly, both my grandparents had travelled several times, mainly by occupying first class cabins aboard various ocean-going liners

My grandmother had travelled both to and from her birthplace in India, the long distance to England and in addition, shortly after her marriage, she had also travelled to Ireland via a second class ticket although that trip did not have the advantages of first-class travel. It may well be that it was because these were early days of the marriage and finance may have been somewhat more limited.

Records also show her to be leaving Ireland with a last known address in Belfast, but there is no trace of her ever having arrived there.

Logic dictates that to leave there, she must have arrived there in the first place, right?

There must have been reasons for her sudden and dramatic departure from India to a destination which was such a long distance away, not only from my grandfather but also from her mother and additionally her sister, who had both continued living in India.

My grandfather had made journeys on his own whilst travelling independently on the various occasions back and forth from India to England and by means of first-class travel, although on separate occasions of course to my grandmother but on some of these occasions on maiden voyages they were literally like ships passing in the night.

These travel plans would have been very expensive as the ships that they journeyed on were fitted out to the height of luxury and so referring to the previous chapter on financial well-being, this does present at least a limited amount of evidence that there were some elements suggesting wealth but not necessarily of his own finance.

There are many records in the public domain evidencing not only the various journeys made but also, stays in the hotels providing the best accommodation or on other occasions in a rented Central London apartment at a particular address in the West End of London for longer periods of time, where he was waited on in the apartment by a man who became his friend.

However, if it was his money, he was entitled to spend it on whatever he chose to at the end of the day.

Although the apartment block has now been demolished, luxury homes have been built in its place. We were in contact with a gentleman who was the son of the owner at that period of time, who had attended to my grandfather.

All of these are facts which have been proven officially from UK Board of Trade documentation and photographs which were taken by us in the 1990s.

The identity that he was known by from the early 1920s was the same one which according to passenger lists, he had used for some of his later trips.

It may well be that because there was now the legal necessity for travel documentation and it was likely that as the name on his passport would need to have coincided with that provided by his naturalisation application, trips to England could no longer be made using his false documents.

We know of the approximate year that my grandfather had supposedly died as he was shown as being deceased on a family marriage certificate, but having researched in India, there is still no physical proof to confirm this date and it is not beyond the realms of the imagination that my grandfather could have invented yet another new name, and had simply disappeared!

Also, the certification that was provided on him could have easily been falsified as the family member may have fallen out with their father.

Miss Y had also stated that she had been informed that a telegram had supposedly been received by one of her siblings announcing the death of my grandfather, but admits to having never physically seen any documentation to that effect. It must be borne in mind once again that this could be the perpetuation of another myth.

Who could or even would have sent a telegram from India and who would have even known about the existence or the address of his English family anyway?

Does this point to the fact that a will had actually been made or had been left – or failing that, some instructions to be followed in the event of the death of my grandfather?

Perhaps it was just an up-to-date address book that had been kept by him in a very safe place or maybe there was just some clandestine contact between the UK and India that Miss Y had not been made aware of?

Once more we have no answer.

Where there's a will there's a way, but at present there is no will so there is no way!

There were also some photographs taken on a balcony in India of my grandfather and his family which would have been taken prior to my grandmother and the children leaving India on either of their trips to England, so in 1932 or 1933. However, my grandfather appeared to look quite a bit older than the age that he was supposed to have been at that time period.

It is of course possible that it was simply that the sun may have aged him a bit but we were surprised at how old he did look, perhaps 20 years older than the age that he was.

There was an additional photograph of my grandparents. Although it has a date written on the back 5 years prior to my grandmother leaving India, they both look at least 10 years older than a picture of them, taken at the time she left for England. If so, this could mean the handwritten date was an attempt to deceive, as a wall in the background appears to be English built going by the scenery suggesting a somewhat older property.

As photographs are not proof of age, it points to the possibility that my maternal grandparents did get together just before World War Two and had actually continued rather than abandoned their relationship.

There were also photographs of my grandfather supposedly taken on the steps of what was said to have been the Anglo-American Club in Bombay and on that one, he does appear to look so much shorter than he did in other photographs.

The question has to be asked as to whether it is him or perhaps somebody else with a similar appearance?

Once again, the information was given by Miss Y, so who knows?

SUMMARY

THE FACTS V THE FICTION

Facts that have been proven

- Date and place of birth
- Name at birth and the names of his parents and siblings
- Family ethnic origins
- Criminal and military record
- Marriage
- Births of all three children
- Freemason
- Travel pattern 1940's/1950's

The Fiction

- Various false birthplaces
- Various false names
- Fake and continually changing of Nationality
- Fictitious military rank
- Unproven early career or financial status
- Unproven death date or location.

PART TWO

MISS Y

Overview

We have anonymised the people featuring in this book so far by changing their real names.

We will continue with this but rather than think of a fictitious name for our next character, we intend to refer to her under the alias of Miss Y.

She was my birth mother but what I wanted was a mum, someone who I could rely on to love and care for me in the way that a mother should.

There are many questions I would have liked answered.

- She walked out on her 9- and 11-year-old girls – WHY?
- She stood by when her third husband abused me – WHY?
- She wouldn't listen when I told her of my distress – WHY?

So, for those reasons, my mother will be known as Miss Y.

A judgement on Miss Y and her honesty or dishonesty can be made after the information provided in this book has been read and digested.

The second part of this book deals with the many somewhat shocking revelations that have been discovered about Miss Y who was the daughter of my grandfather, and had from a rather young age lived a life of lies and deceptions.

What our research has uncovered is disturbing and also extremely unpleasant, although it does need to be said that the information discovered proves to be very informative for those in the family, who are interested in finding the true family facts which have been concealed up to now.

It has all proven to have been a very interesting exercise, because of what has been uncovered on both my grandfather and also Miss Y, continue the theme of deception, destruction and deviousness.

My grandfather appears to have passed on his art of deception to his daughter. Miss Y appears to be following in her father's footsteps but in a deeper and darker manner. Whilst she may have thought that she could get away with her many deceptions, nothing could be further from the truth, a phrase that could be regarded as very apt, based on her personality. Although, this can only be through example set rather than time spent with him, as she had quoted that 'she had seen him infrequently', having spent a minimal amount of time or contact with him during her whole lifetime.

In my opinion Miss Y has been unbelievably wicked in many of her ways since her early childhood, and only got worse as time has progressed.

The family myths that have been passed down the line by Miss Y herself with the likely intention of making her own birth right seem far grander than it really was at that time. Therefore, she would appear to be much more exciting and to superficially appear more attractive to the outside world, but especially to the male population of that outside world.

Miss Y has always sought to make her life appear far grander than it was and been happy to exaggerate and enhance by making things up for her own personal advantage or by stealing the identity, property or husbands of others, purely for her own self-satisfaction.

That was the way that Miss Y had always operated and probably always will.

CHAPTER 1
MISS Y AND HER EARLY YEARS

According to Miss Y, my grandfather and her appear to have spent a very limited amount of time together in each other's company. As such, the assumption could reasonably be made that he'd had little influence on her life.

Therefore, the old saying *'like father, like daughter'* would not apply because he had no influence on her upbringing and so no bearing on how she had chosen to live her life.

Yet, from what we have been able to discover to date, based on information found on various items of paperwork we have, Miss Y not only became a carbon copy of her father, but she has also displayed traits of dishonesty seemingly much worse than my grandfather.

As you know, my grandfather had been living on a more or less permanent basis in Bombay (now Mumbai) in India from around 1918 as a result of his transfer from the British Army to the Indian

Army Reserve. Although Miss Y had originally been born in India, she had emigrated to England from India along with her mother and one of her siblings before she had reached her 2nd birthday.

Well into her middle age, there had been very rare travel events occurring for Miss Y. Any travel she had pursued did not involve journeys to or from India or the Asian continent and had been at a much later time in her life compared to my grandfather and so, they would not have met up.

When he had made what had by now become regular trips for him, between 1948 and 1954 from India to England via steam ship, he had tended to stop over in England for a six-month duration on each one of these occasions which has been verified by the information found on passenger lists as these confirmed both arrival and departure dates.

He had visited various temporary locations during his stays in London and if that was the case, why did my grandfather and Miss Y not see each other on a more frequent basis over this six-year time period?

It is of course possible that my grandfather had spent some of his time in Ireland if the rumours of buying and selling racehorses were correct, although to date this is an unproven factor.

My grandmother and her children, as has been mentioned, lived at many different addresses after their move to England but never seemingly long enough to settle in or stay at any of them for a long time period. The various locations include a number of London addresses, Farnham and Kingston in Surrey, as well as the Channel Islands. They eventually settled in the seaside town of Worthing in West Sussex.

They had almost certainly stayed there to give the children some stability of education, although even whilst living in Worthing, they were housed at several different addresses, before it could be claimed that my maternal grandmother had finally ceased her nomadic life.

The Worthing addresses we have identified are legitimate as they have been found in various directories, of which there were quite a few.

Although the full addresses are not supplied for privacy reasons, this is not vitally important in the book as the contents focus mainly on the lives of my grandfather, Miss Y and myself and these facts just give some extra information on the family life.

The younger family members had boarded at their various private schools during term times, in and around London, Hampshire and Worthing, as well as in Shropshire during the War years.

We have some school information and paperwork relating to family members, partly provided by other relatives but also through contacting the school archivists on a direct basis ourselves.

Some of these schools are no longer in existence so further information is unlikely to be available now, although we do have some interesting records already.

The children spent the rest of their free time and school holidays at home before and after term times with their mother and the various siblings.

This private education had been presumably provided and funded by my grandfather but it is not possible to be 100% certain on this aspect.

The money that had financed this expensive education appears to have been taken for granted and wasted by every one of these extremely fortunate individuals, who did very little with their education in terms of a career or profession.

In fact, all that appears to have been gained from this education is that they looked down on those less fortunate than themselves, seeing them as being beneath them, so a very bad attitude towards people in general.

What makes them so special and above those less fortunate than themselves?

The simple answer to that is absolutely nothing.

Why did their schools or more importantly their mother, not ever teach them any good manners on how to behave?

This failure to instil at least some family values into them in the time that they had spent at their boarding schools or at home may have led Miss Y down a spiralling path of dishonesty and immorality later in life.

Her female siblings had also fibbed and some of them had also cheated.

Everyone is equal and private schooling does not and should not change that.

In fact, to have a private education is a privilege and '*you do not educate to segregate*' at any time.

It also appears to be a case that there had been little discipline at the schools either and yet the teachers must surely have been in a position of locus parentis, but who knows?

Maybe some of the pupils simply took advantage of the system?

Initially, Miss Y was educated at a private Catholic school in London during her early years in the mid-1930s.

Later, she and some of her siblings were educated at another Catholic school in Worthing.

Miss Y had admitted that as a young girl she had stolen from the collection plate at one of the convent schools that she had attended. She had explained that she would pretend to put some money onto the plate but with a sleight of hand take that and more cash back out. She would do this by attracting the supervising nun's attention by apparently tickling her feet.

So, in other words, Miss Y was stealing by distraction, as opposed to stealing by attraction, as became the case in her later life.

Later, as an adult, Miss Y had said that she was quite proud of stealing from the convent collection plate and the ingenious way that she had managed to do it.

She had found it highly amusing, although honest people would regard it as being unacceptable, appalling behaviour and of course dishonest.

In a church environment, the phrase 'thou shalt not steal' is a commandment and should have been borne in both thought and deed, but Miss Y's main commandment at the time seemed to have been 'don't care, won't care,' without any thought or consideration for anyone other than herself.

Whilst Miss Y was living in the Farnham house with her mother and siblings, the awful news arrived one day of their eldest sibling's tragic and untimely death during World War Two.

Miss Y gained some work experience at a very famous department store in Worthing, Sussex, where she lived. She worked on the cosmetics counter.

She claimed at a later time that her mother used to drop by during her working hours in a drunken stupor and had shown her up in front of her colleagues, but whether this was true, who knows?

Another relative suggested that Miss Y herself had been accused of stealing at that store.

She had managed to secure a job there as a Sales Assistant before she very suddenly and unexpectedly relocated elsewhere for a fresh start.

This could have been due to the suspicions of theft piling up against her, as she disappeared from Worthing in the same way that my grandfather had disappeared from his own hometown in America during his times of thieving.

By all accounts, Miss Y seemed to be a troublemaker from childhood which in the eyes of the law as had applied at that time, was until she had reached the age of twenty-one years old.

She had refused to recognise any authority and whenever challenged anywhere or at any time, Miss Y would simply disappear or run away from her problems rather than face up to them.

She disappeared from Worthing prior to her coming of age on her twenty-first birthday. Whilst she may have still been a child in the eyes of the law, she was not a law-abiding citizen.

As she was under twenty-one years old at the time, authorities would not have been able to prosecute her as an adult as the law would have treated her as a juvenile.

She disappeared to Chatham, Kent. She couldn't go far but she went the distance to a dockyard town, again near the sea, and appeared to have met a male companion who will be known by the initial B for now.

It has been described anecdotally that my maternal grandmother along with one of her sisters, pursued Miss Y to Kent, attempting to try and persuade her to return home. She was clearly mixing with various undesirable people at the time, unsurprisingly mainly of the male genre.

The real truth is that if the facts about Miss Y were relayed from myself to any of the current family members, they would not be accepted by the majority of this family due to their mistaken belief in the good character of Miss Y. She could be extremely convincing but she was in reality, a compulsive liar.

They would believe naively that her lies were plausible even if they would literally bear no resemblance to the actual truth. Miss Y could come across extremely convincing and even appear credible to her listeners. It appears that she must have received some sort of pleasure seeing people suffer at the expense of her own deceit and lies although usually to gain some personal benefit.

She would of course deny this, but then liars do deny and have no conscience at all, nor generally show any remorse.

My grandparents had other daughters, one who was obviously a sibling of Miss Y, and, according to Miss Y, in possession of many of the true facts regarding ancestors but unfortunately, had stayed mainly tight-lipped on things so the degree of truthfulness is unknown.

As an example, when I had asked for some family information which was at the time required for one of our own children's school project, Miss Y had replied that she had no information and suggested that her sister, my aunt, be contacted as she was the only person who would have been in possession of the facts.

However, the response was neither helpful nor enthusiastic as the maternal aunt suggested that the request for the information required be written formally, listing all of the details of the information required.

A ridiculous request when this was a direct family member and especially as there wasn't enough time to even send the questions, let alone receive the reply back in time for the project to have been handed back into school.

Miss Y was so nonchalant in her attitude as though nothing and nobody else had ever mattered but then they rarely did to her. She used other people's kindness and good nature to take advantage of them in every way possible and to gain every opportunity that could arise from it.

She had lied, cheated, and deceived people who she knew and who generally trusted her including employers, her own children and other relatives, her husbands on multiple occasions and she had many infidelities and affairs during her various marriages.

Of course, even my grandfather didn't stoop that low but then my grandfather didn't necessarily cheat.

It was purely Miss Y who had made those allegations about her own father being a cheat, but then she had barely known him, so who was she to judge him?

It is up to the reader to make up his or her own mind once the full contents of this book have been read and absorbed.

Dealing with another and separate subject there were supposedly, photographs in the maternal family allegedly dating back several generations. All photographs are important but in the terms of family history research, can be vital for proving and disproving theories. A picture paints a thousand words, but equally, so does a photograph!

However, who the photographs related to, if they even existed has not been confirmed as it was said that they had been damaged by smoke and water in a fire at the home of two nieces of Miss Y. Maybe this was yet another smokescreen rather than smoke damage as nothing would surprise?

Whilst I would always have been interested in any of these photographs, purely for family history purposes, I really do wonder whether they had ever existed?

Did they really get damaged? I am simply not into playing games and so I am not going to worry about it and intend to draw a line under the whole incident.

What is strange though is that the newspapers of that time do not contain any report of any such fire as ever having occurred at the address concerned in Brighton?

Strange but true.

Photographs can be seen as quite an important part of family history as seeing can be believing. The whole of the maternal family were exceptionally secretive about the supposed family photographs amongst many other things and does it matter anymore?

CHAPTER 2
DALLYING WITH
DRUGS

After Miss Y had moved away from Worthing and following on from the fruitless attempts of my maternal grandmother to return her to the family home, it is known that Miss Y had a boyfriend in Chatham called Brian.

It is strange that even many, many years after the relationship had finished, Brian used to visit her at least once every year whilst he was staying locally, usually in Southsea regardless of which address she was living at, in whatever part of the country, regardless of the distance he had needed to travel.

This continued for many years after she had moved away elsewhere in the country and a long distance from Chatham and the general Kent area.

The fact that this had happened must mean that they had both mutually stayed in contact with each other and kept their addresses updated at the time.

Numbering each boyfriend enables me to work out who is who but the exact order in which these males were dating Miss Y may be slightly askew. Then I had never asked the exact order because I knew that the answer would be that Miss Y wasn't sure herself.

When I had asked Miss Y about Brian, she was told that he had been an old boyfriend but that he was nothing serious.

But then of course by now I had the feeling that the same answer applied to anyone, except Miss Y herself.

Where or when Miss Y had met Brian is unknown, apart from somewhere in Kent, and Miss Y said that she could not answer the question as she couldn't remember.

When she was asked about Chatham some years later, this caused Miss Y to erupt in anger, but as things have unravelled on details, I now know all or at least most of the answers to my questions, as to the time she spent in Chatham and most other places by doing my own research.

Quite early on during her residency in Chatham, Miss Y had worked as a barmaid at a public house. It was only a short time later that she would have met her by now deceased second boyfriend who will be referred to as Roger, which is not his real name.

It is not certain whether Roger was a customer in the pub or whether the pair met elsewhere, but they did go on to marry.

So, she had acquired her first husband or at least the first husband of her own that is, as opposed to someone else's husband.

Roger married Miss Y in October 1952, a few months after she would have celebrated her 21st birthday as she was by then officially regarded in the eyes of the law as an adult.

So, she was now responsible for her own actions including getting married without parental consent being needed.

We have purchased a certified copy of the marriage certificate which shows us the full details of the marriage to ensure the details were correct.

The seemingly happy couple then lived in rented accommodation for six months and this would then take the time through until about April 1953 by which time Miss Y had, it would appear, become fed up with her new-found married life and also bored with her first husband Roger, so presumably he was little more than just a passing fancy.

Whilst Roger was working hard at the cinema, Miss Y was cheating on him by projecting herself onto another man, who at the time was also married to somebody else although he was separated from his wife for reasons that will be described later.

He also lived in the same rented house as Miss Y and Roger whose days as husband no. 1 already seemed to be under threat.

The new man in her life will be referred to as Kelvin. As mentioned, he was already a married man, and also was known to the police by the nicknames of *Morphine Mark* and *Mark the Pedlar*.

He is no longer alive but appears to have been a no-mark though, as we will demonstrate later in the book.

As stated, he had been lodging at rooms in the same house where Miss Y and Roger were also renting rooms from a Professor and his wife at their Chatham house.

The reason that Kelvin had not been living with his wife, according to his now ex-wife's own personal statement which she made to us, was that they had been previously living as a married couple in her mother's house.

However, Kelvin had been serving a stint in prison for theft and drug dealing and because of the dubious company he was keeping at the time in question, he used to sometimes sleep with a loaded gun in his bedside drawer.

He used to boast that he was a member of one of the organised crime gangs in the East End of London opposing the Krays during the very early 1950s and so he had felt the need to protect himself.

However, he couldn't protect himself from his mother-in-law and she simply evicted him, as she refused to have a convicted drug dealer living in her house which is quite understandable, given the circumstances.

To evidence this aspect of the story of Miss Y, *The Chatham News* had printed the following story in May 1951, naming Kelvin:

A married man, Kelvin Sanders known to the police as Morphine Mark, now aged 22 who at the time was living in Napier Road, Gillingham, has been sent to prison for two months.

This was after he had pleaded guilty to stealing a bicycle from outside Gillingham Grammar school and had also asked for three other offences to be taken into consideration.

These were the theft of hypodermic syringes from All Saints Hospital, Chatham when he worked there and in addition, to the theft of a drilling machine and two dozen lenses from another place of employment, although in that case it was from an employer's premises in Rochester, Kent.

Later the same year, *The Chatham News* also reported an update on this story on Kelvin to the effect that:

> *Morphine Mark now aged 23 but still living in Napier Road Gillingham has been remanded in custody at the Bow Street Court, London charged with breaking into All Saints Hospital, Chatham the previous April and stealing dangerous drugs.*
>
> *He was further charged with feloniously receiving heroin and other drugs as well as an automatic pistol, knowing them to have been stolen and with being in unauthorised possession of dangerous drugs.*
>
> *The Court heard that he had left his address and was now of no fixed abode.*
>
> *The first hearing was adjourned and when the trial recommenced evidence was given by a hospital employee as well as detectives from both Chatham and Scotland Yard and the case was transferred to the Central Criminal Court.*

The criminal trial then commenced in October 1951 and *The Chatham News* headline and the full details of the trial were splashed across the pages of the newspaper.

GILLINGHAM MAN WAS KNOWN AS MORPHINE MARK

The trial took place at the Central Criminal Court at the Old Bailey and the jury heard that Kelvin Sanders had stolen a large quantity of drugs from a Chatham Hospital and sold them to drug addicts in the West End of London, where he became known by the nicknames of both Morphine Mark and Mark the Pedlar.

Kelvin had pleaded guilty to breaking and entering a store at a Hospital in Chatham and stealing 1,000 half grain tablets of morphine sulphate as well as other drugs and to being in unlawful possession of dangerous drugs.

Before he was sentenced to two years in prison, the prosecution had told the court that a large stock of dangerous drugs consisting of Morphine, Heroin and Cocaine had been stolen and that the defendant then proceeded to hawk the drugs around the West End.

The police evidence was that he was spotted with a number of men and two women who were recognised as drug addicts. Mark was questioned and taken to West End Central Police Station where he was found to have on him two phials of morphine and a phial of heroine.

He made no reply when he was asked where he had obtained the drugs. Morphine Mark also had two *holdalls which contained another seven phials and an automatic pistol.*

When he was asked where the pistol had come from, he had told the police that he had bought it more than three months before for £3 10s 0d. In his statement he had explained that at the time of the break-in he was unemployed and had no money.

After stealing the drugs, he had initially hidden them in his garden and later in a bedroom, but then decided to go to London to sell them.

He had said that he had the idea that coloured men might be interested, he had approached a couple of men in Charing Cross, London who in turn had introduced him to other people and because of that, he said he had been selling these drugs to them four times a week.

His statement went on to say that young girls of nineteen had also approached him and he would charge them 4 shillings for a half grain tablet of heroin, explaining that he did this because it was easy money.

When the police had searched his Gillingham home, they found more drugs in a bag.

One of the detectives told the Court that Morphine Mark was asking for one other offence to be taken into consideration, concerning the theft of the drugs whilst he was employed at the hospital in 1950.

The Court also heard that the defendant was a married man but living apart from his then wife and that there was one previous conviction at Chatham for stealing a pedal cycle.

After he had come out of prison for that offence in June 1951, he had been unemployed, although the Court also heard that at one time, he had served in the RAF with an excellent character.

However, he had also told the police that he had been taking these drugs himself.

The defence told the Court that after he had left the RAF, he had obtained a post at the hospital as an assistant dispenser with the intention of qualifying as a pharmacist.

His lawyer added that the strain of working long hours and then studying until 2 or 3am got too much for him.

To help cope with his difficulties he had got hold of a drug similar to Benzedrine which had helped him to cope for a time but constant use resulted in the drug losing its effect and so he began taking something more potent, gradually becoming a drug addict.

His wife then told him that she wanted a divorce and he threw himself back onto drug taking.

His explanation was that such was his craving that he conceived the idea of breaking into the hospital *and rifling the drug cupboard stating that at that time he had no intention of peddling drugs in the West End.*

The Police Officer advised that at the time Kelvin was a slave to these drugs and that he had said he was bitterly ashamed, but he had friends who were willing to help him overcome his craving.

As he passed sentence down, the judge said:

"You are your own enemy, perhaps your own executioner, although that is something which need not happen at all, for while there is life there is hope. But no man can play with fire and escape. That is what you have been doing. Prison may be your salvation."

What was confusing however was the quantity of drugs that had been stolen as referred to in the above Chatham newspaper article.

The reason is that in a Birmingham newspaper in 1951, there had been an article relating to the break-in at Chatham which Kelvin Sanders had pleaded guilty to.

The offence had taken place on the previous day to the report being published and this referred to the haul consisting of 3,000 heroin tablets, 2,888 Diamorphine hydrochlorate tablets, 2,600 Morphine Sulphate tablets and 4 x ½ oz bottles of Morphine Sulphate powder.

This adds up to considerably more than the 1,000 grains of Morphine Sulphate previously referred to.

Interestingly, *The Chatham News* in the same month as the Birmingham article mentioned, confirms the exact same quantities of drugs but also commenting that the police believed that the thief would have had a knowledge of drugs.

Kelvin Sanders as evidenced by his police nicknames of Morphine Mark and Mark the Pedlar was a very bad boy in every sense of the word and he was described in the *Daily Mirror* newspaper dated October 18, 1951, as selling heroin and cocaine drugs to teenage girls on London streets and the article referred to him as a street peddler.

So, this is the delightful man for whom Miss Y had just deserted her first husband of only six months to shack up with.

The actual date as to when Miss Y had met Kelvin originally is unknown but presumably it must have been after he had served his time in prison and if that was the case, perhaps it was during her stint as a barmaid? Perhaps it had been that Miss Y had been playing with fire but then she appeared to like the excitement, or otherwise boredom would kick in.

Maybe it was before Kelvin had been sent to prison and Miss Y was waiting for him to get out of prison before they could then go ahead and make their plans. Perhaps it was no co-incidence that Kelvin had taken rooms in the same house as Miss Y?

As the affair developed between the pair, Miss Y and Kelvin eventually fled from their lodgings in the Professor's house in Kent and they moved on to another dockyard town along the coast at Portsmouth in Hampshire, where they set up home together in a rented flat in Old Portsmouth, deliberately and falsely pretending to be a married couple.

To evidence this, the same address was also mentioned during 1954 but the facts surrounding this appear later in the book under the newspaper headline *Shopgirl Regrets.*

During the early 1950s, physical proof of a couple being married was then a requirement before they could be accepted as tenants anywhere as living together. Unmarried couples would not have been regarded as morally acceptable by any landlord or landlady.

However, Miss Y and Kelvin had a way of getting around that so called problem, despite being unmarried, and that was by using the stolen ration book of Kelvin's now ex-wife with Miss Y falsely posing as her, taking on her full name in order to match what was shown on the book, so as to make their relationship appear legal.

So to summarise, Miss Y was now living with a drug addict who was also a hardened criminal with multiple drug and theft convictions himself.

Kelvin who it will be recalled, was also known as Morphine Mark had stolen drugs and needles in their previous dockyard town of Chatham and had sold them on in London as well as having been found guilty of the heinous crime of stealing a bike.

Yes, a pedlar in more ways than one!

He had served his time for these offences which were widely reported in various national and local newspapers at the time.

After the relationship between Miss Y and Kelvin finally ended, he eventually moved on but he had then remarried in England and subsequently emigrated to America.

It seems that he had not discussed his previous criminal history with his second wife and that she had been completely unaware of anything that had happened whilst he had been living in England.

Obviously, because of the history of drugs, the American authorities might have expelled him from America had they known and he could not take that risk.

The question that has to be asked is how did Kelvin manage to enter America with his criminal record relating to drugs?

Another conundrum.

Despite having been married to him for a number of years before his eventual death, Kelvin's second wife was completely unaware of his past and he had never divulged any facts ever to her.

That was until an advertisement from his second wife had been placed in the Portsmouth News a few years following Kelvin's death as she wanted to make contact with anyone who had known him prior to their marriage.

We didn't see the advert and so cannot verify that what we were told was even factual, but Miss Y had said that she had seen the article and responded to the appeal for information at the time.

The question is what was supposedly said to Kelvin's second wife and was it fact or fiction that was provided? Probably a combination as Miss Y would not wish to incriminate herself.

CHAPTER 3
PORTSMOUTH
& GOSPORT

The couple, Miss Y and Kelvin Sanders, had originally met and started a relationship at their previous residence in Chatham. They had stolen Kelvin's wife's ration book for the purpose of using it to evidence a false identity in order to obtain their accommodation.

Indeed, they used it for anything else that was required for himself and Miss Y, including no doubt to obtain his ex-wife's rations in addition to Miss Y's own allocation of those goods that were still on restricted supply.

It seems that Miss Y had inherited at least one trait from my grandfather – the ability to create a false identity to obtain a pecuniary advantage.

Other relatives of mine have also stated that Miss Y and Kelvin Sanders were said to have stolen large quantities of brass from Portsmouth Dockyard during the hours of darkness with the assistance of a boat. It turns out Kelvin was a boatman. Maybe the old saying that 'where there's muck there's brass' should be reversed to 'where there's brass there's muck'?

The story was that these exploits had been reported in the "News of the World" but unfortunately, this title has not yet been digitised by the British Newspaper Archive and so it has had to remain unverified.

Presumably, though, Kelvin Sanders was by now becoming rather boring for Miss Y.

It seems that he was no longer wanted by her or perhaps he could no longer provide sufficient funds to finance the desired way of life of Miss Y.

Perhaps the element of the original excitement of being associated with a wanted man was no longer there and therefore he was discarded just as Roger had been.

Kelvin continued with his stealing and had also carried out other crimes both whilst he was living with Miss Y and after their relationship had ended too.

To evidence this, a few years later, the *Portsmouth News* reported that Kelvin was up in front of Portsmouth Crown Court charged with and subsequently being found guilty, along with three other men, of planning an armed robbery at a Portsmouth garage.

The next boyfriend for Miss Y was number 4 and was named Ronald but who is also now deceased. This was becoming a longer chain reaction than even Diana Ross would have been proud of but having said that, Miss Y had nothing at all to be proud of regarding her chain reaction.

Miss Y had cheated with Ronald on not only Roger to whom she would still have been married to at that time, but also Kelvin, with whom she was still living at the time in the capacity of common law wife.

After Ronald she quickly moved to her fifth boyfriend, to whom we won't give a name on this occasion but who was to eventually become her second husband, on whom she would cheat with Ronald in repeated torrid sessions of adultery, despite the fact that she was still married to her second husband. The strange thing was that it was Ronald who had originally introduced Miss Y and her second husband to each other.

He had set them up on a date with stories to him of her promiscuity, all whilst she had still been living with Kelvin! At the time that Ronald had introduced her to her second husband, it was said that Ronald had told him that if he wanted to sleep with her, 'She will sleep with anyone.'

This story was told to us by her second husband who, whilst being an honest and decent man, fell for this seemingly inadequate and deceitful example of a female.

How Miss Y didn't become confused by all the men in her life is beyond most people's comprehension!

I had managed to track down Kelvin's first wife for a chat some years ago and was able to gain some background information as to Miss Y's earlier time with Kelvin. What she had to say was very interesting as she was more than happy to give many details about his life as a gang member, so far as she could recall.

One almost amusing anecdote was that he was known to the girls down the dance hall as 'Norbert' because as they put it, he was nor but a lad!

I had mentioned that the pair had stolen her ration book and she was then rather concerned to learn about Miss Y impersonating her.

A few years later, we received a telephone call again from another of Kelvin's relatives who had also spoken to Kelvin's ex-wife, who in turn had passed our contact details on to him.

As a result, he had some questions of his own to ask about Kelvin's past, which was not a problem and we were happy to co-operate, but again, we were provided with some useful, additional information in return.

One of her later, and possibly the most deceptive of her affairs was the one involving her sixth boyfriend, who was shockingly also one of her brothers-in-law.

It is likely that this affair occurred over a period of several years, as although Miss Y herself confessed to the liaison having taken place, she referred to a different time period to the one that had been recalled by other relatives, who had remembered the episodes exceedingly well, which perhaps is not surprising.

It isn't clear as to which one of them started the disgusting affair, but that makes no difference – they should have stayed away from each other, not only for the sake of their families but simply because it was immoral.

Either one or the other of them, or probably both, should have known better than to cross the rather obvious thin line of sleeping with someone to whom they were related through marriage.

The harm and pain that was caused that was so avoidable, not least because of the immorality and deception, but additionally because of their family connections and the pain it naturally would have caused to their other halves.

It would seem that there was little or no thought given to other family members but seemingly, Miss Y displayed no morals and had no guilt about anything or anyone in her quest for carnal satisfaction. She was by now quite experienced in cheating, seduction and deception.

She has caused a lot of very unnecessary tension between other relatives, which continued over some years and they were of course innocent parties in this situation. Yet, she always caused devastation as she was a troublemaker.

Miss Y always acted as though she was the innocent party and had done absolutely nothing wrong. This false belief and bad attitude could not be any further from the truth.

Another one of Miss Y's male friends, boyfriend 7, made trumpets. It turns out he 'just wanted to be a friend' and yet they were observed kissing outside Miss Y and her husband's home at Privacy Place in Gosport, and in full view of her husband, publicly taunting and humiliating him in front of other friends.

This was sick and totally unacceptable.

The facts are that Miss Y appeared to enjoy collecting husbands but in many of these cases they were other women's husbands in addition to her own.

Despite by then having been married to her second husband for some years, Miss Y was still sleeping with Ronald, who, it will be recalled, had originally introduced her second husband to this despicable example of a woman.

Ronald still appeared to be hanging around Miss Y like a foul smell then and for many decades following, too.

These affairs with Ronald sometimes took place at the house of someone known to Miss Y, but the owner may have been abroad at the time.

The house where this adultery took place was close to the cemetery at Gosport and occurred on various occasions whilst Miss Y's husband was at home in the evening with their two young children.

Her husband had his suspicions raised regarding Miss Y so unbeknown to her, he had arranged for a babysitter for a short period of time and then walked around to the house concerned as this was less than a five-minute walk away. He was able to clearly observe Ronald and Miss Y through a window in a compromising position.

Having realised that the game was up, Miss Y knew that she had been caught out, she turned into a blacksmith and made a bolt for the door, running through the back door in her attempt to escape.

She didn't stop her affair with Ronald, though.

What special element did Ronald have, or what did he have on Miss Y, more likely?

Let's go back to the man on the front garden wall.

Miss Y has always maintained that a relationship did not take place with him, but only because he refused to make music with her. Allegedly, this was because he did not want to get involved with a married woman.

However, it didn't prevent Miss Y continuing to pursue the musician and dreaming about what could be done to encourage him at a much later date. She has confessed that on multiple occasions she had attempted to seduce him but without any success.

On a later occasion, the musical friend apparently even asked Miss Y for some relationship advice on his then girlfriend, which, as quoted by Miss Y, had riled her somewhat.

Miss Y had repeatedly lied, cheated, and tormented her husbands with many different men over the years and this was cruel on any occasion and morally wrong, but she clearly enjoyed what she saw as her having control.

The next man to come into her life was in 1965, while Miss Y was still married to her second husband.

This person we will call John. He was her 8th boyfriend.

The subsequent divorce petition obtained by her second husband stated that this sordid affair lasted for a few months.

Miss Y did admit to her adultery with John – plus, he was a married man, meaning he was someone else's husband.

Miss Y took a break away, literally, and headed off to Scotland for a weekend away with John, on the pretext that she was staying with some old married friends, who had at the time – in the 1960s – lived in Marble Arch, London and she had used them to give her an alibi.

Miss Y had at the time of needing an alibi mentioned to these old friends that she had needed a favour but whether they had turned her down or whether they agreed to cover for her on that one and only occasion is unknown.

As a result of this I knew, having checked out the details, that one of these supposed old friends had passed away, unknown to Miss Y; yet he was supposedly an old friend.

She had used them as she had so many other people, and then had dumped them.

Her husband had once again become suspicious and visited these old friends to ask whether she really was visiting them, only to find out that she was not staying with the couple,

This affair, as we said, was mentioned in the later divorce allegations against Miss Y.

Her husband had said that he had decided to forgive Miss Y for this sordid episode, even though it was not her first affair, to protect their children.

However, we do have in our possession a copy of a Solicitor's letter addressed to her husband which would have been written during this time.

The letter refers to the mortgage on the family home being transferred from their joint names and solely into the name of her husband by joint agreement.

It would seem to be that this had been part of the agreement for her second husband's forgiveness to transfer the title of the family home into his name only, which seems to be a very smart move on his part.

This was done so that if Miss Y was to re-offend at some future date by once again cheating on him, which incidentally she did, then if their marriage ended, she would have no claim on the property.

Miss Y told her children on a later occasion that she had wished that she had claimed her half of the home from her ex-husband despite the fact that she had signed a letter from a Solicitor some years previously giving up her rights to the house. So, she had even *lied* to her own children. How low can a person sink?

Wherever Miss Y went or had been a trail of lies and destruction followed.

CHAPTER 4
CRIME TIME

In addition to the marriages and the cheating with a series of boyfriends, Miss Y had carried out many other deceptions during her lifetime, including many criminal activities.

But then this is Miss Y, the daughter of my grandfather.

Her father, my grandfather, had been convicted of theft and embezzlement and had tried to avoid jail time by stealing someone else's identity.

Miss Y certainly followed in her father's footsteps, but she hadn't just stolen somebody else's identity, but many other things. Was she a magpie who couldn't keep her hands off anything that was shining brightly or that she was attracted to?

She managed to get herself a job by using the fake identity of Kelvin's first wife, gaining her employment at a large chain of chemists. She continued to use the false identity from the stolen ration book that was mentioned earlier.

Miss Y had resorted to stealing from the till at the chemist where she worked, but when she was caught and charged with embezzlement, she had maintained the fake name that she had been employed under and so when she appeared before the magistrates at Gosport, the subsequent conviction was *not* in her real name but had instead been recorded against the name of Kelvin's ex-wife. This lady has now been made fully aware of what had happened and was quite understandably extremely upset. She subsequently went to a Kent Police Station for advice, but the police were able to reassure her that it would not count against her.

It does not in any way make this right though as any acts of theft, especially and including identity theft are simply wrong

This theft was reported on page 8 of the local newspaper, the *Portsmouth News* in the summer of 1954 and the following is a full transcription of the article in question:

SHOPGIRL REGRETS

Smartly dressed in black, a shop assistant admitted to the Gosport Magistrates today that she had abused the position of trust in which she had been placed.

She was under the name of Josephine Sanders (22) of Old Portsmouth, who pleaded guilty to embezzling

from Timothy Whites and Taylors Ltd separate amounts of £4s 6d; £8s 10d and £10s.

She was conditionally discharged for 12 months on payment of 25 shillings costs.

Inspector G G Gates said that the company employed a firm of professional shoppers to make test purchases at their store at 127 High Street Gosport.

The accused did not record on the cash register the full amounts of the purchases.

Sanders told the Court – "I am really sincerely sorry about it.

I am quite sure it won't happen again.

I don't know what made me do it.

I was trusted all round in my job.

It was a very nice job and I am sorry I let everybody down."

Alderman J A Wheeler (presiding) said :

"The Court feels you have been very foolish."

Also adjudicating was Mr C B Blake

The newspaper reported the facts of the case and her possibly insincere apology to the court.

She had been placed on probation but afterwards she had continued offending, so when she said 'sorry', what she probably meant was 'I'm sorry I was caught'.

Nearly some 70 years later, she is still known by an abbreviated version of the first name of the person on the ration book and rarely by her real name as was shown on her own birth and baptism records, apart from when she spoke to her nieces and reverted to her proper birth name.

So even at this late stage of her life, she is still touting her false identity.

As was stated above, we were able to track down the real person named on the ration book some fifteen years or so ago and telephoned her, not knowing what sort of reaction, we might receive.

However, she was more than happy to discuss and freely provided us with a considerable amount of very useful information, filling in a lot of gaps in the early days of Miss Y and her previous life in Chatham.

The ex-wife was very informative regarding the time that she had been married to Kelvin Sanders and we truly thank her for those facts as they have certainly helped to present a balanced report on the circumstances, as opposed to what appeared to be the complete work of fiction that Miss Y had supplied.

At least we now have more facts on Miss Y prior to leaving Chatham for Portsmouth and running away with Kelvin.

In addition to her conviction for embezzlement from Timothy Whites and Taylors Ltd in Gosport High Street, Miss Y had also offended on several other occasions.

Miss Y has told us directly that whilst she was working at a bookshop in Gosport High Street sometime after 1957, she had been stealing from the till. She was caught by the owner, who had noticed that the takings were down on several occasions when he tried to balance the takings.

He decided that one of the shop assistants must be stealing and had decided to put a special red dye on the cash, and as a result, Miss Y was literally caught red-handed!

Perhaps never say dye could have been Miss Y's catchphrase at that time.

She was of course immediately dismissed from her employment but the proprietor was otherwise lenient and did not report her to the police, so Miss Y got away with her theft quite lightly on that occasion.

Miss Y herself had said that many years later, she had returned to the bookshop and said that she had apologised to the owner, but our view is that this is extremely unlikely to have happened.

The business of Timothy Whites & Taylors Ltd had been taken over by Boots the Chemist and when I had on a later occasion applied for a job in Gosport, Miss Y informed me that she had stolen money there several years previously and so she was sure that my application would not be successful.

I am unclear as to whether she was referring to the theft when she was using a fake identity or whether there was a further incident or incidents of thieving, as frequency is unknown.

However, much to Miss Y's surprise, I did get the job, but always had the feeling that the supervisor on the cosmetics counter was watching me closely to ensure that I was not following in my mother's footsteps, which I wasn't and never would.

However, I simply went about proving that I could be trusted and that I was the honest character that my supervisor hoped that I was.

I even became friends with the lady at the time to the degree that I was invited to and attended her wedding, which took place in 1974.

However, the criminal activities of Miss Y continued unabated and there was a major incident towards the end of the 1960s when Miss Y had at the time been employed as a part-time shop assistant at a Gosport gown shop.

The shop was located at the far end of a shopping precinct in Gosport, not more than a few hundred yards from where she was living at the time in the family home at Privacy Place, Gosport.

The trouble was that everyone in the immediate locality was aware of the gossip and had eagerly passed on titbits of news to their neighbours.

How Miss Y could carry on as though nothing had ever happened in front of the other householders in the local area and anybody else is unbelievable!

The shop was named after the owner who was a lady called Mrs Williams who is now sadly deceased.

Miss Y had at the time stolen money and goods and used her 'Timothy Whites' trick which was that if a customer entered the shop and bought something, Miss Y would charge them the full price and take the right money.

However, Miss Y would then ring up the sale at the till with a lower price and then she would pocket the difference.

So, it was a case of deceit without the receipt, the same as it had been for the thefts from Timothy Whites and Taylors. She seemed to have no shame or to have appeared embarrassed by her wrong doings, but just quoted that 'it was over and done with and in the past'.

Mrs Williams had become suspicious after her accountant had alerted her to the fact that there were obvious stock shortages and so she had decided to begin watching Miss Y very closely indeed and had caught her literally with her hands in the till.

However, unlike the bookshop owner a few years previous, Mrs Williams had no hesitation in calling the police or in reporting Miss Y who was in due course charged with her crimes.

Miss Y then appeared in person at Gosport Magistrates Court.

We have several documents relating to this court case and Miss Y was formally charged at Gosport Police Station in the late 1960s that:

> *You being a person employed in the capacity of servant in the employ of Mrs Williams did between 1st February 1966 and 9th October 1967 at Gosport steal £150 in monies belonging to the said Mrs Williams contrary to Section 17 (1)(A) of the Larceny Act 1916.*

Miss Y was then charged in 1967 with a second more serious offence which was that:

Between the 1ˢᵗFebruary 1966 and 9ᵗʰOctober 1967 at Gosport, being a servant to Mrs Williams, you did with intent to defraud, omit from a till belonging to the said Mrs Williams, your employer, a material particular, namely, the total sum of £150, from customers, contrary to Section 1 of the Falsification of Accounts Act 1875.

At the time of being charged with the offences, Miss Y was released on bail in the amount of £10 and instructed to attend the Magistrates Court in Gosport, two weeks later on the 26 October 1967.

At the Magistrates hearing, Miss Y admitted to the offences but at the same time, had also disclosed her previous 1954 embezzlement conviction, although on that occasion she was charged under her false name of Mrs Sanders, but had obviously forgotten that!

She was however remanded on bail yet again in the sum of £10, pending medical reports.

She was then free to come and go, waiting for a further summons from the Clerk of the Court to attend at a further hearing to continue with the trial.

THE PORTSMOUTH EVENING NEWS carried the following story:

£150 THEFT BY SHOP WOMAN AT GOSPORT

A Gosport housewife admitted at the Borough Magistrates Court today that she stole £150 while working as a part-time shop assistant.

Miss Y (under her real name at the time) who admitted a previous conviction for embezzlement in 1954, was remanded on bail for 3 weeks for medical reports

Mr J Bates for the prosecution said that [Miss Y] had been employed from February last year as a part-time assistant in a Gosport gown shop.

In September this year, he said the Proprietress realised from her Accountant's report that there was a discrepancy.

She kept a watch on [Miss Y] it was alleged and saw her charge a customer 7 shillings but ring up only 4 shillings and 8d on the till.

When challenged [Miss Y] was stated to have admitted taking amounts which she estimated totalled £150.

Calculating the value of money in late 1960s against 2023 values, the current equivalent of that £150 exceeded £2600. This must have been a fortune for the poor lady who owned the shop.

The Court set a date for a further hearing for the following month, but in the meantime, ordered Miss Y to undergo a Psychiatric Medical Examination and to attend Knowle Hospital in Fareham.

The hospital subsequently sent her a letter dated 27 October 1967 advising that she would be an in-patient at their Unit in Fairfield House, Droxford, Hampshire, where a bed was being made available for her on the following Monday.

The letter from Knowle Hospital Management Committee in Fareham supplied a list of articles of clothing etc. to take with her:

- *1 dress or skirt and twinset*
- *3 prs stockings*
- *2 prs pyjamas or 2 nightdresses*
- *1 coat*
- *1 pr slippers*
- *2 sets underwear*
- *4 handkerchiefs*
- *1 dressing gown*
- *Toilet requisites, writing material, stamps, etc*
- *Please note that this list includes clothes worn.*

It would be appreciated (Except in exceptional circumstances), if the sum of money you have with you does not exceed £5 - 0s - 0d

The hospital investigations had clearly found Miss Y to be of a sound mind and not mentally impaired in any way.

At her next Court appearance a few weeks later, she was put on probation for two years and ordered to repay the £150 that she had stolen at a rate of at least 40 shillings per week.

She was also ordered to attend a psychiatric outpatient's clinic during the first 12 months of her probation, for further assessment.

Unfortunately for poor Mrs Williams and her disabled husband, the compensation was of little comfort and it was too late to save their business.

As a result of this cruel act Mrs Williams became bankrupt, according to an elderly friend, and a near neighbour of Miss Y at the time, who was also quoted as having said that 'the court case had been utterly horrible for the couple.'

The Gosport Gown shop is nowadays a fish and chip shop so that gives an idea as to its location.

The reimbursement order meant that Miss Y had to begin looking for another job for her to pay off the compensation award that had been imposed against her by the Court.

She found a job at a local Public House and begun working there as a barmaid in late 1967.

It will be recalled from her marriage certificate from her first husband Roger, that she had some previous experience in bar work from the time she had lived in Chatham, around fifteen years earlier.

Another opportunity for Miss Y to get out and mingle.

Whilst Miss Y was working in the public house at this time she met a punter who became her ninth boyfriend. He was called Mr Macaw.

He was another married man, somebody else's husband!

He eventually went on to become her third husband and had been a regular customer at the public house where she worked.

Several years later, a relative had informed me that Miss Y had been suspected of stealing money out of the till at another shop where she had worked, at a later date.

Despite having been put in a position of trust and placed in charge of the shop, it appears that Miss Y betrayed the owner's trust for her own benefit yet again!

But then Miss Y seemed to only care about herself.

CHAPTER 5
YET ANOTHER
AFFAIR

Miss Y was not the best example of a mother. Her children did not appear to matter enough to her in her single-minded world of deception and selfishness.

According to the eventual divorce petition, her second husband had no option but to stay at home in the evenings in order to look after their children while Miss Y earned money to pay the required compensation.

It was Miss Y who had been caught stealing from Mrs Williams and was therefore required to pay back her compensation award by earning an *honest* wage, an alien concept for her, perhaps?

As a result of his baby-sitting responsibilities, her husband had been unable to give Miss Y a lift either to or from her new workplace and after a while, it was brought to the attention of her husband, in addition to him noticing himself, that she was always being given a lift home by car from the same person, Mr Macaw.

The ludicrous reason that Miss Y had supplied to her husband when challenged as to why this man was regularly giving her lifts home in his car, was that it had been because at that time, he was unable to collect Miss Y from her workplace in Gosport on the evenings that she had been working as he was being a decent dad, looking after their children and it would have been irresponsible of him to have kept them up late or left them even for a short period of time on their own as they were still of a relatively young age.

However, her feeble excuse had been that she was too frightened to walk home alone into Privacy Place as it meant that she would have needed to pass by the local cemetery in Gosport at night. Given that she was a barmaid, she should have been used to dealing with spirits. In all seriousness, all she would have needed to do was to cross the road to avoid being on the cemetery side. But of course that was not the reason for not wishing to walk home alone.

Mr Macaw had in what appeared to be a kind gesture, offered to give Miss Y a lift home.

The cemetery story is now known to be a complete fabrication, of course and was just a cover up for extra-curricular activities with Mr Macaw. In his statement to the divorce courts when he was named as co-respondent, Mr Macaw had admitted that despite knowing that she was a married woman he had still continued his antics with her anyway.

No doubt he had an ulterior motive and thought that he would get payment in kind in return for giving her a lift, which of course he did. Their scenes of affection were often observed by the close-knit community, and the information was fed back by neighbours to her husband.

The road in Gosport where they lived may have been called Privacy Place, but it was certainly not a private place. But then Miss Y had been seen up to her old tricks very publicly and in the company of Mr Macaw, so what else could be expected in the circumstances.

Shortly after her husband's suspicions had been aroused, he arranged for a babysitter to look after the children one evening and he followed Miss Y and Mr Macaw in his car, after she had finished her shift and they had left the public house.

However, instead of going straight home, they drove to a seafront car park at Gosport and had parked in a bay, clearly part of their clever plan to avoid the cemetery...

Her husband had seen enough and after having observed the cheating couple in a compromising position, he returned home repulsed and in despair as he knew that his marriage was about to finally come to an end.

When Miss Y later arrived home, he tackled her about what he had seen earlier and she admitted that she was *fond* of Mr Macaw.

Given that the Court had set out a minimum rate of reimbursement to Mrs Williams and the repayments commenced in late 1967, Miss Y would have completed the payments at some point in 1969. Yet it was now in the middle of early 1970 and Miss Y still continued to work at the Public House in Gosport, even though it was no longer necessary for her to do so.

In other words, she seemed to be avoiding being at home except for a short time period.

As she was the mother of two young children, it must be questioned in which direction her loyalties and sense of any responsibility lay, even if the answer is a fairly obvious one.

This was in 1970, and very soon after this incident, Miss Y left her husband and her children by her own personal choice and admission, having been given an ultimatum by her husband to end her affair for the sake of the children.

However, Miss Y chose to reject her husband and children in favour of Mr Macaw and went to live with him at another Gosport address. He would eventually go on to become her third husband.

All this is evidenced by the facts contained in the divorce papers filed by her second husband at the time, shortly after her departure from the family home.

After her husband's suspicions had been aroused and Miss Y had rejected his offer of reconciliation, they did eventually get divorced. Her husband had no option but to petition for a divorce on the grounds of her admitted adultery with Mr Macaw who would soon be up in front of the Beak.

So, Miss Y had dumped yet another man, and this time the father of her children. This was an act of meanness and proved that she was simply self-centred to the extreme.

Miss Y appeared to have no concept of truth, feelings or love and seemed to discard men and anyone else she no longer required like a cigarette butt.

Miss Y has always maintained a collection of the phone numbers of her many current and previous male friends and stayed in touch with them even if they were married and had placed their contact details into her address book.

In addition, as they had gradually passed on, she then stayed in contact with their wives even if they hadn't felt comfortable with this.

It certainly can only be seen as a weird and bizarre obsession of hers, whereas most other people would be content in collecting stamps or coins. It seemed almost as if these men were reserves for emergency purposes as and when required by her in the event of a break in her supply chain!

Most decent people at least attempt to make the right choices in their life, but if they go off course, many of them would normally change their direction and correct their path.

However, it appears that Miss Y presumably preferred the excitement and thrill of staying off-course, enjoying the bumpy ride that went with it.

It seemed to be a bad habit of hers that couldn't ever be broken, but it was nobody's choice but her own to always be on a continuous trail of self-destruction.

As one of her own remaining relatives was quoted as saying:

'Miss Y was common by her own choice, became common by choice and would remain common by choice as even her education could not and would not get her out of this one!'

But the past does catch up and becomes the present. The saying *be sure the truth will find you out* applies very aptly to Miss Y.

She has had a large input on this aspect and she would prefer to be sketchy and brief to try covering up the many lies of her own in the same way that my grandfather had done nearly 50 years previously.

In the same way that my grandfather had deceived his direct family by lying and covering up about his past, everything in Miss Y's world was disguised to give the illusion of grandeur and so she appears to have clearly followed in my grandfather's footsteps in this way for completely different reasons. It seems that she had delusions of wealth.

Miss Y was quoted as saying all that she had inherited from my grandmother was an old coat with a chicken wishbone in the pocket, presumably suggesting that she needed 'good luck' in her life. In fact, what she really needed to do was to simply change her self-centred ways and her outlook, particularly towards other people.

The wishbone would not change the Miss Y ways as this leopard will never change its spots not now and not ever.

It was clearly a generous and kind offer from her mother having given her the old coat and wishbone as she really doesn't seem to deserve anything.

MALE COLLECTION SUMMARY

1	Brian	Chatham
2	Roger *(the first husband)*	Chatham
3	Kelvin *(the drug dealer)*	Chatham
4	Ronald	Portsmouth
5	??? *(the second husband)*	Portsmouth
6	??? *(the brother-in-law)*	Drayton
7	??? *(the trumpet player)*	???
8	John	Portsmouth
9	Mr Macaw	Gosport

PART THREE

MYSELF

OVERVIEW

Part Three of this trilogy relates to myself and demonstrates how the negative actions of Miss Y have caused a massive impact throughout my life.

We have heard about the chain of thieving carried out by Miss Y but the biggest theft of them all was her self-centred and inadequate behaviour towards me, the lack of nurturing and genuine affection that should have come from and been shown as a natural part of motherly instinct, but this is something that has simply never materialised over the years.

The lack of interest shown from a mother along with the constant rejection, had been illustrated by other parents as they collected their children from school. They would give their children a hug, which just added to my pain and disappointment as I usually had to walk to and from school alone as a young child. Sometimes however, I would have been collected from the playground by my Nannie who had always shown affection towards me.

I learnt to keep myself to myself and not to ever ask any questions as otherwise my natural childhood curiosity would simply be rejected by my mother, as she was always simply too busy.

My father, by total contrast, was a kind, caring and genuinely lovely man who hadn't a clue what his wife was like. However, I was a young child and found it impossible to speak out or attempt to get the words down on paper. But now, they are in writing.

Miss Y stole any confidence that I had, and more importantly prevented me from developing an ability to trust other people, both male and female as a result of her actions and inactions, as will be shown later.

The huge impact on my life generally but also on a far wider scale due to a more sinister cause, the details of which I will describe in a while.

I was considerably shell-shocked whilst still a child growing up at the unpleasant facts that very slowly unravelled before my very eyes but have also been revealed to me from both paternal and maternal sides of the family and additionally by the various contacts of Miss Y.

I knew that I would need to obtain physical proof of what had been said to me, as evidence was essential if I was to be believed. If I found some of the information to be unbelievable, then how could I expect other people to believe me?

Having learned to always expect the unexpected I was extremely surprised by the sheer volume of the deceptions, lies and cover ups that have come to light.

I hope that by telling my true-life story as it has unfolded from the beginning to the current time, then it might just help others in similar situations to myself to understand and believe that they will eventually come out the other side, albeit with a few scars and war wounds. They need to know that despite the best attempts of some people to make them feel inadequate and useless, that they are neither of these things. They are survivors.

Repeatedly being put down by an adult who you should have been able to trust implicitly can result in a child believing they are inadequate, when it is not the case.

CHAPTER 1
MY EARLY YEARS

I am a survivor of Miss Y's cavalier and disinterested attitude towards her parental or any other responsibilities, but also of other, far worse matters mentioned later in this part of the book.

Miss Y seemed to have become the person that her very own side of the family refer to as 'common,' rejecting any of her family values, including any benefits of her private schooling which she herself had stated was very enjoyable but also her upbringing, changing her voice from being well-spoken to seemingly become loud or even vulgar by her own choice.

It had been a very difficult home life for me and whilst my father was superbly kind, loving, caring and trustworthy, he was like most fathers of the 1950s to the1970s, working hard all day. And as the saying goes, 'whilst the cat's away the mouse will play!'

As a result of the negative attitude continually demonstrated by Miss Y, I very quickly became accustomed to being ignored or pushed away when I was young.

I was singled out and then had been bullied at school due to the fact that I was a shy, quiet and withdrawn child.

Bullying first occurred in junior school from around the age of seven years onwards by being threatened and excluded by my peers or through hitting, kicking, and being pushed away.

As I got older, school time for me became much worse and by the time I had started at senior school at eleven years old, the bullying accelerated and the threats became worse along with the singling out which was very unpleasant despite my best efforts to get myself included.

I was also mocked and picked on for no apparent reason as well as being jostled and kicked during school hours. I would be followed and threatened with beatings on my way home.

This continued throughout my school life as I found no reason to change my quiet personality for those bullies, and so I attempted to ride it out.

By the time I was in my early to mid-teens, life at home slowly became unbearable as will be explained later.

Additionally, I would try to avoid school and had walked out of the school gates because of two separate classroom attacks which had involved a boy forcing me into a music room cupboard and attempting to rape me, fortunately without success.

This was when I began to avoid school to stop these assaults and also to prevent the threats of beatings both on the way home as well as during school hours. I felt that I was a target due both to my quiet personality and because I was petite in stature and size.

The problem was that I felt that there was no-one to turn to or to confide in, but then unfortunately, there wasn't.

As I got older, I was also continuously being harassed, insulted and put down at every opportunity by Miss Y, over whatever I had worn clothing wise, my hair style or lack of make up as I was growing up from being a teen to becoming an adult.

Even later in my adult years, if I had visited Miss Y while wearing sportswear, either on the way to or returning from the gym, or as part of a recovery programme following a hysterectomy as the result of an endometriosis diagnosis, I would be greeted with a reaction of general disgust, suggesting that perfectly decent attire should not be seen or worn in public.

Being told that my clothing was unsuitable and that I looked like a tart hurt me and caused considerable upset. It did nothing for my confidence.

It hadn't mattered whether it had been a skirt or a dress, whether they were above or below the knee, Miss Y criticised and mocked me. Whether it had been a blouse or a high neck jumper, criticism was fired at me, and to be honest, even if I had been wearing a bin liner, I felt that I would still have received the same reaction.

A little understanding from a parent, particularly a maternal one who a daughter should have been able to look to for guidance or to show an interest, can go a long way to assist in positivity, but unfortunately the maternal side was not pleasant, supportive or understanding, and positivity from Miss Y or anyone on that side of the family had never existed.

Any positivity, encouragement or support came from the paternal side only.

I strongly believed in marriage and all that it stands for, and having observed many wrong situations, didn't plan on ever making the same errors or misjudgements that Miss Y made again and again. The importance and sanctity of marriage was something that had been played down in a very negative manner by Miss Y and several of the other females on that side of the family too. These relatives seemed to look down on me for no apparent reason.

As a result of this, I promised myself that I would never follow their example in any way.

I did not steal other people's property or husbands, nor did I practise deception, do crime of any sort and have never taken drugs either.

I have never cheated on my husband, and won't ever, as I have seen the effects on my father and the suffering that was caused to him by the cheating and the continuous lies from Miss Y.

Also, because the Miss Y side of the family, had never seen marriage as being sacred, loyalty or faithfulness has simply never been important for any of them.

I have fully researched the details of my father's education and that is noted privately and offline on the family tree and will stay there with the rest of the information that is noted.

I am rather pleased that I haven't been educated through the Catholic religious system even though I have been baptised and was later confirmed and married as a Catholic. However, that was based on naivety and not knowing any difference regarding my religion.

It seems wrong that anyone can attend a confessional box, say a few 'Hail Marys' and you are allowed to get on with your life, whatever sins have been committed. It makes no sense.

This is not meant in any way to offend anyone, but circumstances have encouraged me to say it that way.

I have nothing personal against any religion. It was just the attitude in general towards marriage and the lack of faithfulness. It always seemed that others on the maternal side could choose any partner and appear on the surface to commit to them, but then they would dump them, and then do the same ad infinitum.

Perhaps it was because Miss Y and her siblings had been privately educated and this in my head seemed to go hand in hand with their seemingly snobbish and conceited attitude demonstrating negativity towards me, along with what appears to be the money-orientated attitude from Miss Y, whether it was connected to personal possessions or finances.

A prime example had been when I had attended the funeral of the elder sister of Miss Y, my aunt, to genuinely pay my respects after she had passed away.

One of my cousins was very unpleasant towards me, treating me with no respect because she had heard a story that I had treated my own mother badly. That was a turn up for the books!

Miss Y had made the choice to not attend her own sister's funeral. It was her own choice, and Miss Y had lied to her niece, saying that she had a bad cold, and could not attend. However, I knew this was untrue as I had seen her the day before when she told me that she couldn't be bothered to go to the service. My cousin simply turned her head away from me with her nose in the air when I had done nothing wrong. She chose to believe what she had been told by Miss Y but in effect, was being disrespectful to her own mother too.

However, I decided that the only way forward was to not waste any more time on this episode or that individual. Clearly Miss Y had been stirring up the pot and causing trouble for me, but the only conclusion I could reach was to try to rise above it and do my absolute best to get on with my life.

The privately educated side on the maternal family never seemed to live in the real world. It seemed that they felt it was their right to enjoy the better things in life, but their attitude at times suggested that people they met were like something unpleasant that had stuck to the bottom of their shoe.

Instead of attending a Catholic school, I had been educated at Leesland Church of England School in Gosport during my earlier years.

Other relatives on my paternal side of the family were also schooled there and from a historical viewpoint, I discovered that my great great uncle was the first head teacher there when the school first opened in 1894.

As mentioned earlier, on regular occasions my paternal Nannie would meet me when I came out of Leesland school, but it was just me and not my other sibling.

It has always been a puzzle to me that I had been the only one who would have gone back to my Nannie and Grandad's house in All Saint Road for my tea, without my younger sibling accompanying me.

However, I knew better than to ask questions as I would only have been knocked back by Miss Y who didn't like questions asked of her.

Although I had always enjoyed the time at my grandparents' house, why was it always just me who would stay overnight and for part of the following day too?

This would occur on a regular basis but as my Nannie was a positive influence on me and it was a retreat for me it would always be quality time that I spent there. It also meant that I would on occasions see other family members on my paternal side, such as one of my aunties or some of my cousins who would drop by from their nearby home.

I have personally interviewed family members on the paternal side. The one thing I had discovered was that you do not always take family history information provided by anyone for granted or as being correct.

Having been told many interesting facts over quite a long period of time, which although was well-meant information that had been provided, it sometimes turned out to be exaggerated or understated although not necessarily in a deliberate way.

Sometimes, family members merely repeated what they had been told or thought they had been told by other relatives.

Miss Y had tried to justify her actions in previous years by saying that what she had done was 'in the past and finished with'.

Her crimes and the many infidelities were dealt with in very much the same way with the standard response being along the lines of 'Well, we all make mistakes, don't we?'

In addition to this, Miss Y had also made choices of her own with many other things, such as choosing to drink heavily, and on many occasions she would be the worse for wear and I would witness my mother throwing up in the bathroom afterwards.

Bearing in mind what Miss Y had said of her own mother's alcoholic history, it seems that she had not learned from her own experiences as a girl.

Things became very sad for me and when there is nobody to place your trust in or ask advice from, it is horrible and scary.

As soon as my father returned home from work each day, things appeared to change and Miss Y appeared to normalise her attitude towards me.

It was as always, a relief for me to see someone who clearly cared and always showed it with a hug and knowing that they had meant it. It was always time well spent when he was home, and of course there was no criticism or segregation, as he always treated myself and my younger sister the same.

When it had been bath time as a child, it had always been our father who had placed us into the bath and settled us down with a bedtime story for the night. It would never be Miss Y.

Some acquaintances of Miss Y had been known to sometimes make comments to me regarding some of the thieving and cheating past of Miss Y, but I was always very wary and would never say anything myself as I did not know the truth of these comments, some of which were very shocking to a relatively young person.

It did however make me even all the more determined to separate the facts from the fiction.

As a child of around seven or eight years old, I clearly remember witnessing on a regular basis Miss Y taking Mandrax tablets to presumably help her sleep.

I had found out the name of the drugs from having checked the label on the tablets myself and also by listening to other people's conversations.

Mandrax it seems is a hypnotic sedative, but commercial production of Methaqualone, to give it the proper name, was halted in the mid-1980s due to widespread abuse and addictiveness.

Mandrax became increasingly popular as a recreational drug and club drug in the late 1960s and 1970s, known variously as "ludes" or "disco biscuits" due to widespread use during the popularity of disco in the 1970s, they were also known as "mandies" in the United Kingdom and work in a similar way to barbiturates.

Apparently, an overdose can lead to nervous system shutdown, coma and death.

Additional effects are delirium, convulsions, vomiting, kidney failure, coma, and even death and as a result, the drug was more tightly regulated in Britain under the Misuse of Drugs Act 1971. (Source: Wikipedia)

I would witness my father finding it necessary to push Miss Y up the stairs from behind, in order to assist her upstairs to bed, as she may have simply collapsed otherwise.

She would be very slurred in her speech, possibly because of the effect of the tablets.

This was something that from a child's perspective was extremely distressing and scary but I have never discussed it with anyone until recently, when talking with my husband about the scenes that I had witnessed.

I felt like I was the adult, but in reality I was just a child and by witnessing these awful scenes I was merely 'on the outside looking in'.

Miss Y would then appear to struggle to get up the next morning. She inevitably overslept with the after-effects of the drugs and would be drowsy, so I would need to make my own way to school, but in any event I would probably have done so anyway as this had become the normal way of life for me.

I had become accustomed to not asking any questions and so had just quietly observed and noted these things happening.

I had never discussed any of these things with my sibling as I had felt that she was too young at the time, and as time had progressed and more segregation between my sister and I had taken place, it seemed to be a pointless exercise.

When I was a pre-teen Miss Y had changed her medication to Valium, but eventually switched to Mogadon tablets and had been taking them for many years, allegedly for the same reason, which was supposedly to help her to sleep, and some considerable time later required weaning off them very slowly.

Mogadon is a brand name of the drug Nitrazepam amongst others and is yet another hypnotic drug of the Benzodiazepine class meant to be used for short-term relief only and used for severe, disabling anxiety and insomnia. More common side effects may include impairment of memory, impairment of motor functions, hangover feeling in the morning, slurred speech, decreased physical performance, numbed emotions, reduced alertness, muscle weakness, double vision, and inattention have been reported.

Unpleasant dreams and rebound insomnia have also been reported.

Nitrazepam is a long-acting benzodiazepine with residual "hangover" effects after night-time administration such as sleepiness, impaired psychomotor which may persist into the next day.

Recreational use of Nitrazepam was unfortunately common even though the manufacturers state that treatment with Nitrazepam should usually not exceed seven to ten consecutive days. Use for more than two to three consecutive weeks requires complete re-evaluation of the patient. Prescriptions for Nitrazepam should be written for short-term use (seven to ten days) and it should not be prescribed in quantities exceeding a one-month supply.

Dependence can occur in as little as four weeks (source: Wikipedia)

However, from memory, Miss Y had obtained a prescription for many years.

Seeing my mother under the influence of these pharmaceuticals was once again a sad reminder to me of what it is like being on the outside looking in on a parent who was not fully coherent.

Only one good thing came out of these memories. Clearly etched on my mind was that I would never, ever take sleeping tablets or drugs of any sort, at any time in my life, and I have been true to myself and have not ever done so.

No matter how tough life could be, I would not resort to covering any problems up or lying about them, which was what Miss Y seemed to do – whenever she faced a situation that she had created herself.

Also, in the Miss Y section of the book under *'dallying with drugs'*, it was mentioned that Kelvin Sanders, one of her boyfriends, had been taking a stronger version of Benzedrine and this in turn triggered another memory in me. I had once asked Miss Y whether she had ever taken drugs during her time with Kelvin and her answer was *'No, just a coffee dreg drink to keep me awake and nothing more'*, which is significant, given the later use of Mandrax, Valium and Mogadon tablets.

I have clearly memorised all of this when writing this book and discovered when researching that it would have been the stronger version of Benzedrine that Miss Y had been referring to which according to the internet, apparently looks like coffee dregs!

I had learned an awful lot growing up as a child on what not to do, but really, I, like many others, should have been too young to be learning those sort of lessons.

Children observe everything that their parents do or don't do and so it is important for parents to take account of good or bad influences on their children.

Taking this medication didn't however have any off-putting influence on my mother trying to attract men.

She has led a life of lying, cheating, deceiving, and tearing lives apart like a hurricane, but there did not seem to be the slightest thought for others; she only ever thought about herself.

At one point she admitted that she was jealous of her own sister, who was intelligent as well as being ambitious and had managed to secure a place at the prestigious Italia Conti stage school. Miss Y said she felt that she was more deserving of the place and has certainly managed to live out her own dramas and stories, but not in a good way. Each to their own it would appear.

Miss Y has tried to destroy me in every way possible, showing limited affection to me as a child. One comment she made to other family members, after I was born was to the effect that I had been the ugliest baby that she had ever seen. Two of my aunts had told me this story on separate occasions to each other and I have no reason to disbelieve this particular anecdote.

Growing up, my father would take me out on occasions at the weekend to give Miss Y some space to enable her to look after my younger sibling, and those one-to-one times with my father were good.

He was never made aware of what went on whilst he was at work, when Miss Y was segregating us girls, treating us totally differently, having her favourite and casting me aside.

Yes, this was traumatising and some memories are extremely difficult to forget.

My younger sibling and I had both at first lived with our father following our parents' separation and divorce. He had always been a kind, caring and considerate man. I have him to thank for showing that he cared genuinely and to help develop me into the person that I am.

He worked hard all day and then did the household chores necessary to look after himself and us children.

The next occurrence to affect me really badly was when my paternal Nannie passed away in the early part of 1970, and as I had spent a lot of time with her, I missed her terribly as she had been more of a mother to me than my own birth mother ever was or ever will be.

This had a major impact on my life and although I didn't know it then, it was the start of a spiralling downwards trend in my life and the catalyst for some really unhappy times.

The marriage between Miss Y and her second husband had taken place in the late 1950s and had begun to break down at some point in the early 1960s.

This was confirmed by their divorce petition in which Miss Y stated that they had married in 1957 and that *'the marriage was quite all right for about 4 ½ years.'*

Miss Y had many affairs taking place in the 1960s, as already documented, and the 1965 affair with John was specifically mentioned in the divorce papers. The statement confirmed that this had lasted several months.

Of course, Miss Y was also up in court then to face her charges of thieving at Mrs William's shop. The compensation awarded by the court had to be repaid by Miss Y as mentioned in the newspapers and also on the other documents that were cited earlier.

Finally, the affair in late 1960s or early 70s when Miss Y had first met Mr Macaw (according to Miss Y's own statement mentioned in the divorce papers) in the public house in Gosport where she had started working in 1968, whilst compensating Mrs Williams, the victim of one of her crimes.

Miss Y wasn't inclined to wait long before having an encounter, it would appear, hence the questioning over late 1960s as to when Miss Y had first met her eventual third husband.

Although the divorce papers referred to this as an 'association' which was the legal term used at the time, it had, in Miss Y's version, commenced a month after my paternal Nannie had passed away in January 1970. However, it is more likely that it was prior to this, possibly even as early as 1968 as suggested above.

In May 1970, just before my twelfth birthday, Miss Y made the decision to finally move out of the family home. It was during the daytime whilst we were at school, and this was also mentioned in the divorce papers. So, a daytime flit rather than a moonlight one!

I remember that day quite clearly, returning home from school and being told by my father that Miss Y had left the family home as their marriage was finally over.

The strange thing is that I recall not being at all shocked and it certainly never devastated me, due to the negative impact Miss Y had on me.

In fact, it had felt almost like a relief which then began to make me feel guilty for something that wasn't even my fault.

Eventually, Miss Y moved in with and later married her next husband, Mr Macaw, her third other half (or should that be her other third?) but most definitely her worse third.

My father came into the bedroom one evening during 1971 to speak with me and my sibling who slept in the same bedroom as me. He explained that he was going out to see someone. My younger sister had commented after our father had left that she was scared and so I had told her not to worry and that I would look after her being a couple of years older and naturally protective, but also of a legal age to be left to keep an eye on my sibling.

I had stayed awake until my father had returned home at around 11pm that evening and I had heard the front door close behind him.

I did not discuss this until much later afterwards with my husband, as it was also possible that a female neighbour had agreed to sit downstairs and was in fact keeping a listen out, even though this had not been communicated.

This did reoccur from time to time and as a result, I had been lacking in sleep for school for a while. But who can blame my father for going out occasionally for a few hours after what he had been through and put up with over quite some considerable time? He was definitely entitled to a social life and it turned out that he had met another woman at work who was also a divorcee and the two of them clicked. She was to move in and a short while later, my father remarried. This was in February 1973 and he was once again happy (even if this was to be relatively short lived as his second wife later also cheated on him).

This was when I would have been in my early teens, but my younger sibling who had taken an extreme dislike to the second wife, resented, objected and protested against life without Miss Y.

Eventually this came to a head later that year when Miss Y announced that she wanted my younger sister to live with her and her third husband, but our father would not hear of the two of us being separated and insisted that the siblings must stay together. It had to be both of us or neither!

My father's second wife then made the suggestion to me that as my younger sibling wished to live with her mother then it would be a good idea for me to also do so in order to keep an eye on my sister and ensure that all was okay.

I reluctantly had gone along with the idea thinking that I was being protective, but in my heart I really did not wish to do so. I really wanted to continue living with my father, where I was genuinely happy.

But I was not self-centred and so went along with the suggestion and had to make a decision that any fourteen year old should not have had to do, as will be seen later in this book.

Miss Y had in the end reluctantly agreed to give in and take both of her children.

This was the beginning of my problems being at home with Miss Y yet again who had at the outset made it clear that I wasn't wanted in the first place.

CHAPTER 2
FAMILY HISTORY

I have for many decades been interested in family history and this had first started as far back as when I was just nine years old when my childhood curiosity had got the better of me.

This was the year when Miss Y had stolen from Mrs Williams and was appearing in court and convicted but that unfortunate and chosen incident would simply be described by Miss Y as *'none of your business'* and was *'in the past'*.

I had originally asked Miss Y about my maternal grandfather whom of course I had never met, as I had been informed that he had passed away prior to my birth.

As usual, I received the unhelpful and negative response and was answered with, *'well I don't know do I'!*

As a child, my natural curiosity or questioning on the maternal family had always been immediately dismissed and swept under the carpet, suggesting to me that there was no family information for her to pass to me.

My ancestry was completely unknown to me and was the proverbial blank piece of paper.

However, I don't ever give up easily and on many more occasions, I attempted to ask questions but each and every time I made enquiries they were as always rejected in a firm and sharp manner.

This only then went on to make me even all the more curious, more interested and definitely more determined to find out something much more detailed. I had never actually communicated this but instead just kept my thoughts to myself.

I eventually succeeded as you will have already guessed, but of course this wasn't information provided by the maternal side of the family but by sleuthing work by myself and my husband, starting thirty years ago, so you can see that the thirst for research has never been forgotten.

Perseverance can certainly pay off!

Miss Y was mentally abusive in different ways, dividing her two children with her lies and deceptions by seemingly playing one off against the other.

I had never forgotten my family history mission as I had set out determined to complete my findings with as many of the facts as possible about my grandfather.

After all, the only information I had been told was that he had been an American and that tiny snippet was sufficient to pique anyone's interest, particularly a young girl.

Little did I know however just what facts would eventually be found out from the secretive and by all appearances, the very private world of my grandfather.

I have gradually over many years interviewed and listened with interest and lightly grilled various relatives (not literally though) to obtain their true stories in person, their versions or perspectives of their family lives from what they had remembered or at least believed that they had remembered of their childhoods.

Their stories of both childhood and adult times, of growing up, school, home life and work all formed part of their history and their memories, including how living conditions have changed such as the introduction of gas street lighting as just one example.

Whatever I had been told, I have always checked the facts out properly and have evidenced everything that had been said especially taking account of the old saying *'as memory fades, recollection increases.'*

Half memories become whole truths, and when an ancestor who was supposed to be a high-ranking Army Officer turns out to be a Private in the Reserve Force, or in another example an alleged Bishop actually turned out to be a non-conformist minister, it just goes to demonstrate just how important it is to verify and document everything that you are told. This then provides proof that theories and supposed events are actually facts, thus avoiding any arguments, or indeed challenges by other researchers, or even family members.

If I could only have travelled back in time, I would have loved the opportunity to have also interviewed each of my grandparents, just in case they were able to fill in any gaps in my knowledge, providing me with any missing information, together with their perspectives on growing up as children and their family lives from Edwardian times going forward.

Sadly, two of my four grandparents had passed away when I was still of a relatively young age with the exception being my paternal grandmother (whom I knew affectionately as Nannie). When I was growing up, Nannie was a kind, caring, loving, and a very discreet lady bearing in mind what has now been discovered. She would have been aware of at least some of Miss Y's criminal activities during her lifetime.

However, she had never bad-mouthed Miss Y, despite the appalling behaviour demonstrated against her own son. Perhaps Nannie didn't really know the full facts of Miss Y's wrongdoings?

Of course, the fourth grandparent is my maternal grandfather, who is still somewhat of a mystery, despite searching on many occasions and employing a solicitor in India. If family members will not communicate, we had to find out without them and the process proved to be very worthwhile and a good learning curve.

I had interviewed my father formally and informally, asking him many questions, and as always he supplied me with very helpful and honest answers no matter how painful it was for him to recount some of his memories. The information assisted me by providing some extra pieces of the missing puzzle. My father was able to supply me with some extra, interesting data relating to some of the Miss Y criminal activities, evidenced through some official paper records and newspaper articles.

Additionally, I have been able to obtain even more detailed paperwork relating to events prior to and at the time of my parents' divorce, which have proven to be extremely interesting and useful. They have been fully detailed in the previous part of this book.

By contrast, whenever Miss Y was asked any questions about her childhood at all, she just replied that she didn't know any of the requested facts, but that would have certainly been either because she would have had other things occupying her mind as she had grown up, such as men or stealing. It could have been simply because she wasn't interested and couldn't be bothered to take an interest in her daughter's research.

She had as usual passed the buck to her elder sibling, with the excuse that she knew absolutely nothing other than the information that her sibling had previously given her. In other words, she blamed her sibling and used her as a scapegoat.

One family story that had been passed down over the years was that my grandfather had been a Captain in the Ghurkha Regiment of the Indian Army and that he had been born in Salem, Massachusetts, which was the fabled home of witchcraft of course.

Neither of these tales were actually true of course, and at quite an early point of my research, I was advised by an authority on Anglo-Indian history at the British Library that it was an impossibility to have been a soldier in the Indian Army unless the applicant was British or Indian.

As my grandfather was an American, he could not have qualified and this remained a puzzle for us for many years until the Canadian subterfuge was unearthed. But although it had been a lie, it did of course then give a presumption of him being British and produced his ticket to join the British Army before his later transfer to the Indian Forces.

The fact is that he had only made the rank of a Second Lieutenant in the Indian Army Reserve and so a long way off the giddy heights of a Captain.

One of the barriers to obtaining more information was that my maternal grandmother had only lived until I was 5 years old and so I had only known her for a very limited time period and I was certainly not old enough to ask her any questions.

Therefore, I had very little information that was available about her too, partly because at that age I was too young to have had the family history interest, and as visits to her residence were infrequent, I didn't get to know her particularly well.

Her marriage to my grandfather and her death and burial details are known partly through obtaining the certification but additionally through visiting the grave and tending to it as well as visiting the funeral directors. They gave us full details of the services for both my grandmother and uncle which were fascinating to read.

DNA testing was one of several key essentials forming part of the research to help finally establish the truth and make that connection to link up with the correct families of each of my grandparents. Genetic testing is a vital part of modern day research and is regarded as an accurate scientific tool.

My father also underwent a DNA test and this was very useful in helping to identify whether relatives were on the paternal or maternal side of the family.

When the research laboratory returned my DNA results, they showed a mixed genetic make-up that was just over a quarter Ashkenazi Jewish, and a smallish percentage of Asian and Viking between both sides of the family, making it somewhat of an interesting mix.

Breaking down the DNA analysis here, the highest amount quoted above includes England and Wales.

The Eastern European Jewish element, clearly from the maternal side from my grandfather and his ancestors, is broken down more accurately depending on the time era. Eastern Europe is an example of a broad spectrum which varies over time as to whether those roots were from Russia, Poland, Lithuania, Latvia or Belarus to name but a few possible territories.

Of course, I would have been a mixture of DNA, broken down through approximately 50% of each parent but not necessarily an absolutely equal amount of the DNA is taken from each parent.

By that, what is meant is that if your parents take a DNA test, there would be bits of each of their parents and grandparents and so not necessarily 50% of each.

The religious facts get more and more confusing as this book has developed though getting the ball rolling on the Jewish side of the ancestry.

Further back through my grandfather's siblings, my own DNA appears to gel nicely into family connections there and is evidence of links in the community based on the DNA results.

Siblings do not always look alike or even similar as their looks, features and even traits, can veer towards one parent or the other or even miss a generation and pick up from the previous generation.

My grandfather had been born in Boston, Massachusetts, USA of Eastern European parentage and Jewish descent, which meant he was 100% Jewish himself, even though he was a first generation American.

Information from the DNA results of me and by my grandfather entering into a marriage in India to a Catholic, following the rites of the Catholic Church, just introduced additional difficulty and confusion through mixed cultural differences.

Then there is the Irish side of the family to consider, with their DNA passed down partly through my maternal grandmother who was a staunch Catholic who had been born in India and was the daughter of an Irish father who had joined the army. He was a Sergeant Instructor and part of the Warwickshire Regiment with a long line of Celtic ancestry.

However, in addition to this, there were also Irish genes on my paternal side of the family.

The Scottish element of my DNA has a slightly higher percentage through the Miss Y influence on the mix and the same applies to the Irish segments, but there is not a significant difference between them.

Where the Scottish ancestors link by way of naming conventions, is yet to be established, but it is something we are working on but almost certainly link in via the Irish connections.

The Asian part of the DNA comes from Northern and Southern India and also features Tibet which comes into play through my grandmother's maternal ancestry.

The final DNA sector relates to Sweden and Denmark through both the maternal and paternal sides of the family, over a much longer time span, so a fair old mixture. But, DNA testing is always interesting to help prove that someone is or is not who they purport to be.

It is especially so when a person gives so many different and varied identities, and who also appears to switch between a variety of different names depending on where he was at the time and of course also who he was as a person.

If we had not carried out previous research on my grandfather we may have assumed that he had 100% Jewish genes based solely on DNA and would have been an accurate indicator to someone who was just starting their research journey. In our case, the results I obtained validated our traditional research and so was extremely satisfying.

One thing that is proven is that because I do not have any Canadian blood in my DNA, therefore his false ID when joining the British Army is exactly that... false!

With my maternal grandmother having been born in India of a Eurasian mother and an Irish father, thus making it perhaps more of an obscure reason to move to England permanently, so the question remains: why move to England after just two short visits to the country? Her Irish family would have been closer distance wise, as her brother (who would have been my great-uncle) had left India for Dublin prior to 1931 and now lived there with his wife and family. It is said, anecdotally, that the relationship between my grandmother and her brother was also one that had broken down but such is the complexity of this family, it is not known when, and perhaps more importantly, it is not known why.

Neither my grandmother nor her brother left India because of the partition, as this did not occur until several years after their respective departures.

So why did they leave India?

Additionally, although her paternal grandparents were both deceased by then, my grandmother would have had a number of aunts, uncles and cousins in Northern Ireland. Miss Y anecdotally has said that she had met her aunt, uncle, and some cousins but that was the extent of the information provided. It is not known whether it was my grandmother and her children who actually visited Ireland or whether the Irish relatives had travelled to England; Perhaps they were already living here on a temporary or even a permanent basis.

Miss Y was convinced that she had three cousins and that one that she specifically remembered went by the name of Geraldine. Our research shows that this information is totally incorrect, however, as none of these cousins went by that name and in any event there were more than three of them.

We do of course have certificates to evidence our proof of their real names and this is all noted on our offline family tree.

We have amongst our documents my grandmother's youngest brother's marriage and his death certificates and we also have other Irish birth, marriage and death certificates relating to the same family, along with many photographs.

Other than locating her return to India from Ireland on one occasion several years prior to her move to England, passenger lists do not show my maternal grandmother travelling out of India beforehand.

In DNA terms, Miss Y is approximately 50% of my grandfather but also my grandmother with her stronger Asian and Irish mix of ethnicity, and no doubt a few other elements as well, which would have been derived through her own grandparents although there may be additional mixtures.

Bearing in mind that ethnicity is not necessarily an exact 50% of each parent, but usually, as we have discovered, is slightly more complex with some extra bits and pieces thrown into the mixing pot for good measure as has been discovered.

Myself and my husband were visiting Ireland on holiday around nine years ago. We hoped we might find something out about that part of the family by carrying out family history research in respect of ancestors that were resident in the Emerald Isle.

There was information already on the families prior to arriving in Ireland – documentation and photographs – but we were hoping to see what else could be discovered, promising to make for a further interesting trip sometime in the future.

What was exciting though was to meet one of the Irish family members at his home in Dublin and then to exchange information with him about our shared family members.

The newly found relatives were quite excited and interested as they knew very little going back more than two generations.

They said that they had a suspicion that there was an involvement with India but they had no facts, and so it was rewarding to explain a little about their lineage knowing that they were facts.

We subsequently uncovered a bit more information and gained a few extra names and made comprehensive notes to add to the family tree to enable more information to be verified by ordering additional certificates. We will never put our family history information online, as researchers do need to learn how to research correctly by doing it themselves from scratch.

Anything asked of Miss Y relating to her parents or any of the family seemed to make her angry, particularly when questioned about a specific photo which appeared to have been taken in Kent, the details of which perhaps may have had connections to her past.

Maybe there are other family secrets that have not yet been uncovered which she refused to discuss at that time.

At one point during my early teenage years, there was a filing box kept on a shelf by Miss Y along with other arch lever binders and filing boxes which I knew were business records and so didn't go anywhere near them.

However, Miss Y seemed exceptionally secretive about the contents of one of these black boxes and would tell me to stay away from the box and to never touch it.

One day, curiosity got the better of me and when Miss Y was out of the room, I decided to sneak a look to see for myself what was inside Pandora's box. It is natural after all that if a young teenager is told not to look inside a box, then it almost guarantees that they will!

After checking that Miss Y was still not around, I quickly opened the lid, lifted the spring retainer inside the box, and to my shock I discovered the first document was a marriage certificate showing that Miss Y had been married previously.

This was obviously a shock to me. I had no idea that there had been a previous husband!

I had started to read the marriage details and was quite engrossed when Miss Y returned.

She immediately snapped at me and then angrily snatched the document box back, placing it out of view in a cupboard, whilst giving me a real ticking off for looking at the private papers in the first place.

It was made crystal clear that I would be in big trouble if she caught me prying again at what she described as her confidential and personal papers.

Following that incident, I had asked Miss Y whether she had any more children resulting from that first marriage to Roger, whose name I had managed to read before I had been interrupted.

Miss Y saw red and reacted angrily again, shouting that it was none of my business. To me, whether I had any siblings that I hadn't been made aware of seemed to be a reasonable question to ask in the circumstances.

Following on from that, I knew better than to ask any further questions, but vowed to find out off my own back.

It seems obvious now taking account of the results of our research that the contents of the box would have included divorce papers and material relating to the criminal past of Miss Y, as well as the first marriage, for which I now have a copy of the certificate and know much more about.

My mother had told me that what I had found was none of my business, but why withhold basic information from your children if there was nothing to hide?

If there had been nothing to hide, I would not have been writing this book!

And the remaining part of this book goes to highlight other reasons for writing it.

Although Miss Y had two children, she seemed closer to my sibling. I don't know why, but the fact that Miss Y only wanted her younger daughter to live with her and her new husband shows it to be the case.

Despite this I felt no dislike or envy towards my younger sibling and still don't. It was Miss Y who manipulated the situation, and children are not to blame for a mother's bad ways.

However, I have reversed the pattern of marital upset, as I have had just one marriage and a very happy one, with a golden wedding anniversary in the not-too-distant future.

I appear to have been the only one on my side of the family who has found true love, and both my husband and I have remained faithful and loyal to each other throughout our marriage. I have been on a happy learning curve since marriage.

This is a trait that is quite obviously not descended from my grandfather or Miss Y but from the paternal side of my family. To genuinely love and care for each other is after all what marriage is all about.

We renewed our vows on the occasion of our 30th wedding anniversary and my husband and I invited a maternal aunt to the party but the aunt had laughed out loudly and commented that their side of the family didn't stay married.

I was quite shocked by the reaction, but having discovered what I have, I shouldn't have been.

CHAPTER 3
TRAPPED, BULLIED AND ABUSED

Marriage was something that had been played out in a very negative way by Miss Y and her side of the family.

As a result of my upbringing, I promised myself I would find the right man, and when I did, I would stay faithful to him.

I did, and I always have and I always will.

Miss Y's crimes and infidelities were all dealt with by her with the same response *'Well, we all make mistakes, don't we?'*

She showed no care or consideration for anyone except herself. And never was this more evident that when her third husband Mr Macaw, mentally, physically and sexually abused me during my teenage years, making my life sheer hell.

Suffering the torments at his hands still haunts me today, with trust issues, lack of confidence, panic attacks and flashbacks.

Macaw was a sexual pervert and a predator who had forced himself on me with no encouragement or willingness on my part, attempting to grope, rape and attack me as well as continuously taunting me on a daily basis during my time at what was meant to be a place of safety, my then home at *The Lair* Public House, the oldest Public House in Gosport.

This evil behaviour would begin prior to me getting up in the morning when this disgusting creep would come into my bedroom before school.

On the pretext of coming in to wake me, he would pull my bed covers away and grope me whilst I was still asleep or before I was properly awake.

I would attempt to use the limited strength I had against a fully grown adult, hanging on by my fingernails as tightly as possible to the bedclothes, despite being taken by surprise on each occasion.

I would persistently say 'No, leave me alone!' on each and every occasion.

When going to the bathroom to have my morning bath, this pervert of a man was always hovering in the background and I would have to run to the bathroom and make sure that I locked the door firmly behind me.

On many of these occasions he would be banging on the bathroom door and would rattle the handle laughing loudly and calling out, 'Will you be long in there? I'm waiting outside!' which only served to increase the terror that I felt.

I would stay in the bathroom with the door locked, trying to compose myself.

Once I had finished in the bathroom, I would wrap the towel around my underarms and a towel around my head, as I would have washed my hair.

Then I would try to prepare myself, ready to leave the bathroom, first by listening through the door to see whether he could be heard and if I could hear no sound, then I would very slowly and cautiously open the door ready to make a run for the bedroom.

Usually, however, he would be waiting hidden in one of the doorways and would attempt to pull the towel away from my body as he mocked me, even though I had asked him to leave me alone.

His behaviour would start up again on the journey to school when my sibling and I would be given a lift in his two-door Triumph Herald.

I would be slapped or touched on my buttocks as I bent forward to get out of the car from the back seat.

After that, I made the decision to walk to school even though it was around a mile and a half, but it was my preference to the alternative of catching the bus unless the weather was bad, as I was quieter than the others on the bus and would often be picked on.

All of this because a sick individual in his 50s seemed to get a kick out of his continual tormenting.

Back home, and despite me checking before going anywhere on the premises, for instance moving from one room to another, going upstairs or downstairs or even trying to leave the house, it seemed that he would pop up from anywhere, but silently, always silently.

He would also frequently conceal himself in the darkness of a store cupboard downstairs where barrels of beer, boxes of crisps and other snacks were stored, waiting for the moment to jump out from his hiding place and attack me, when I least expected it.

On the odd occasions that as a young teenager I had gone there to fetch a packet of crisps, as I was of short stature and petite, I needed to stand on top of an upright barrel to reach into the crisp boxes which would usually be on the higher shelves.

Macaw would come up behind me and attempt to grope me through my clothing, and as I would be standing, balancing on the dimple shape of an upright barrel, I would not be able to move quick enough as I may have fallen and hurt myself.

After I had managed to get down from the barrel, he would laugh, whistle and try to block my way before finally letting me out of the storeroom.

The experiences would always leave me very shaken.

I was very scared and would have wanted to run to a place of safety but as nowhere was safe, I would just sit in the corner of my bedroom with the door closed firmly behind me, with tears flowing uncontrollably and a garment muffling the sound of my crying.

There were many other separate incidents in different locations but always on those premises, which were supposed to be a haven where I should have been safe.

Sometimes he would expose himself to me too. On the first such occasion, I had been in the sitting room watching TV and was aware that Macaw had come in and had sat down on the other side of the room. I tried to ignore his presence but having heard a noise as he stood up, lookcd up and realised he had unfastened his trousers and had started to pull them down. I tried to get past to escape but he grabbed me and with the other hand, tugged at my underwear. Fortunately, he half lost his balance and I was able to make my escape. There were other events which are simply too horrible to disclose.

On other occasions by the store cupboard, he would unzip himself and just stand there grinning at me.

It felt unsafe and terrifying living at *The Lair* and this was made far worse by a long and fairly narrow, badly lit passageway on both floors, making it scarily dark in places.

Because of the many doors, some of which were locked, the corridors began to feel like places of no escape and gave me the impression of being trapped in a long tunnel of sheer hell.

I am still reminded of these feelings in the current day and is the reason that I get panic attacks whenever I find myself in a narrow corridor or enclosed space in any building. This has been caused by Mr Macaw, the pervert and Miss Y, his uncaring wife.

For a vulnerable female in her early teenage years, it was exceptionally frightening and has caused me great distress.

In no way had I encouraged this sick, despicable male who continuously hounded me in his deviant ways on any occasion he was able to.

However, when I had tried to say something, anything or to ask for help and support or to try to explain to Miss Y, my supposed mother, about the ordeals at the hands of my evil stepfather, Miss Y simply switched off and usually responded by saying that she was far too busy to bother with such things and rebuffed me.

In her mind, there was never a right time. She didn't want to know and certainly didn't demonstrate that she either cared or wished to hear anything that might disturb her relatively comfortable lifestyle.

I tried confronting Miss Y on several different occasions, but each and every time my pleas would be rejected. I was stunned by her negative reaction as she did not wish to hear about it. On the first occasion that Macaw had exposed himself mentioned above, she was in the hairdressers and I ran to the salon crying. Her reaction was 'you'll have to wait until later, I'm busy!'

On the solitary occasion that I did extract a reaction from her, she replied, 'Well at least you weren't raped, were you? If not, then what is all the fuss about?'

She still didn't want to know anything about my sheer desperation at the hands of my evil stepfather.

Miss Y would not offer any support to her distressed daughter like any so called 'normal mother' would do, if their child was in a dangerous situation of abuse.

Her choice was to simply turn her back on me, ignore the pleas for help and simply close the door on the matter, pretending that nothing abnormal was occurring.

I cried a lot but silently curled up with a garment or a towel over my mouth to try to muffle the sound of my sobs.

I felt alone, unsupported and that I had no one to turn to.

This has left a massive and lasting impact, causing me to feel rejected, not just because of Miss Y's reaction but also because it was yet another rejection from her.

As a result of this, I would stay away from *The Lair*, and often I would not return home from school until much later in the afternoon.

I would then go out again after tea, just walking around aimlessly for hours on end on my own, just to avoid being in his vicinity, as I knew that more attacks were inevitable.

I began staying off the premises whenever possible to simply avoid contact with Mr Macaw and Miss Y.

I also skived off school as on separate occasions I was assaulted in a school stationery cupboard, prior to the teacher arriving for the lesson.

So now you know the real me: feeling scared, vulnerable and totally bewildered by incidents that have actually occurred to me through no fault of my own.

There was nowhere safe: not my home at *The Lair* nor at my school during the early to mid 1970s, the two places that should have been places of shelter and security.

It could be scary and potentially dangerous being out unaccompanied on the streets of Gosport until late at night as often drunken sailors from one of the naval ships moored in Portsmouth Harbour would be roaming the streets on long pub crawls, looking for female companionship.

However, it was my perception that this was a safer environment than being at home with Miss Y and her creepy, perverted, child-abusing husband in a place that represented sheer hell to an isolated underaged girl.

Running was the only means of escape from *The Lair* at that time, but nowhere was safe and there was nobody to protect me from the nightmare of my private hell.

Having always pushed my stepfather away and rejected any advances, these attempts continued daily and were very frightening, sickening and traumatic on every single occasion.

Sometimes the only warning that I would get would be when I heard the sound of his awful tuneless whistling or the sound of his feet tapping as he came down the corridor.

This was my horror from hell, and to this day the memories of the attacks still haunt me.

This living hell went on for a couple of years, day in and day out and was very, very frightening as there was absolutely nobody to tell and nobody to trust.

Where was Miss Y while all this was going on?

Out shopping, getting her hair done, or in the mornings recovering from a hangover brought on by tots of brandy each night in the bar of the pub.

She was often the worse for wear with her brandy consumption, but witnessing my mother throwing up in the bathroom as I was attempting to get ready to go to school did nothing to improve my perception of the place, always feeling trapped with little or no chance of escape.

At the back of my mind was the worry that if I reported it to the authorities I might have been placed into care and there were already enough stories in the newspapers reporting on the ill treatment of children.

When I was at school, I was aware that some of my fellow pupils were resident in a children's home and their tales of a horrible life did nothing to improve my confidence that I would have an improved lifestyle.

To the outside world, Mr Macaw appeared on the surface to be a pleasant man, a typical pub landlord, laughing, joking and drinking with his customers, but the real person had a very dark and perverted side. He was a child abuser.

Quite a few years later, my sibling admitted that although there had been no attack on her, she had been aware of Macaw trying to peer through her bedroom keyhole but as a result, she would ensure that it was covered over with her dressing gown.

This had never been mentioned before.

It all became too much for me. When there is nobody to turn to in your life there is a sense of being very alone, and overwhelmed, with no support.

The pair, Miss Y and her perverted sick husband, had mocked me in front of customers who just assumed that I was rude and moody, when I was actually scared and avoiding any contact.

Many years later, according to Miss Y, Macaw had supposedly confessed to abusing me.

But I never ever received any sort of apology or any sign of regret or remorse from either him or Miss Y and so I have serious doubts here as to whether it happened or if it did, whether it was said with any sincerity.

Miss Y's direct comment when I had tried again to explain, even when I was an adult and had been married for quite a number of years, was, 'Well what do you expect me to do? I can't leave him as I wouldn't have any money'.

She merely said that she couldn't leave him for financial reasons, but the real reason was that she wouldn't.

A real mother would not have had to ask what she should do in those circumstances.

When Macaw eventually passed away, Miss Y, without any discussion and despite knowing my feelings, placed an obituary in the *Portsmouth News* on behalf of all of the family and named me personally, saying how much he was loved and missed.

I was completely devastated by this sick newspaper notice which was the ultimate betrayal by Miss Y, nothing less than a stab in the back and the final straw.

When approached, Miss Y simply and shockingly responded that she had to pretend on the surface to *his* children that she had cared for him when in fact, she admitted it was to enable 'her' to inherit, so that there would be no challenge to the will!

She then just got on with her life and continued to simply not care for anyone except herself, it appears.

This is after all Miss Y, who preferred to live a lie.

Even now, more than 50 years later, I still find it exceptionally difficult to trust both males and females because of the physical and sexual abuse I was subjected to at the hands of my evil stepfather, and the mental and sometimes physical abuse from my own mother, and the way she continuously failed and refused to want to listen or protect me.

The physical abuse when I was slapped in the face on several occasions and also hit on my backside with the spiky side of a hairbrush.

I am always slow to trust as, on many occasions, having started to trust a person, I would be let down time after time after time.

Outside of our two lovely sons and daughters-in-law, my only exceptions to the rules on trust are my husband, my father, my nannie, my father-in-law, and my father's third wife, who is one of the kindest ladies you could ever meet.

Added to this short list are some very genuine friends. One lives in Gosport and the others are a second cousin and her husband. I send my love and thanks to them all, even though some are looking down from above.

My nannie is one of those who has unfortunately passed away but I wouldn't have wished her to have known about the unpleasantness that occurred since her death, with my parents having separated and divorced.

CHAPTER 4
HAPPIER TIMES

Once I had started full-time employment, I eventually went on to meet the man who was to become my future husband (Mr Right) and we began dating.

In 1975, we got engaged and although I had not left home Macaw's behaviour seemed to slightly reduce. He was less overt in his actions and would closely brush past me but I was always on my guard because of the history of abuse. I was working full time at an insurance company office in Portsmouth and would spend time at my fiancé's parents' house and he would sometimes stay at *The Lair*. So perhaps it was just that there was a lot less opportunity.

Problems of a different sort arose, though, as a result of the reputation locally of Miss Y and her previous inappropriate criminal and immoral behaviour that had occurred during the time that she was still living with the family at Privacy Place, Gosport.

There was an ex-neighbour from Gosport called Ann who was living there at the same time as

Miss Y had been appearing in Court. It seems that Ann passed on details of Miss Y's bad reputation, which had become public knowledge. Much of the neighbourhood and the rest of Gosport were now well aware of the lack of moral and honest behaviour demonstrated by Miss Y.

Ann was now living and working on the Isle of Wight, where my fiancé lived. Unfortunately, Ann worked with a close future relative and shared this gossip which was then believed by this relative of mine.

This then put doubts in her mind as to my own honesty and integrity values as the relative wrongly assumed that I might follow in my mother's footsteps and turn out to be a case of *'like mother, like daughter'.* As a result, she concluded that I may not make a suitable wife for my future husband in case I followed in my mother's philandering footsteps.

This future relative gave me a really hard time and a lot of heartache and I have always felt to have been under close examination for many decades, making me feel completely and utterly inadequate.

At times life became unbearable despite my innocence over any wrongdoings.

I found it exceptionally difficult to accept and to cope with the relative concerned and the accompanying criticism, as I should at least have been given a chance to prove myself and be judged on actions as opposed to having been pre-judged.

This has once again made me feel very uncomfortable and I have always felt that the unacceptable behaviour on the part of Miss Y throughout her lifetime appeared to be following me.

I had done absolutely nothing wrong at all and would always be staying loyal and faithful as I was blissfully happy with my boyfriend and by then, my husband.

Meeting my future husband in the office where we had both worked was when I learned what genuine kindness, caring and, eventually, love, were.

A revelation here to demonstrate the differing attitude of my father and Miss Y was that within a few days of learning that I had a boyfriend, we were both invited to tea by my father. He suggested that my boyfriend, as he still was at that stage, went with him to take the dog for a walk. During that time, he asked pertinent questions about my boyfriend's ambitions, family and attitude generally. He didn't quite go as far as asking if his intentions were honourable but this did demonstrate just how much he cared for me and was simply being protective.

By contrast in the two-year period up to when we got married, neither my mother nor stepfather ever asked any questions or took an interest in my wellbeing.

The trust element was something that developed slowly and gradually over a long period of time.

Although we fell quickly and deeply in love, it felt right, as I really loved someone who was the complete opposite in his personality to that displayed by my child-abusing stepfather, Macaw and what had been so negative in my past.

When my fiancé and I did get married, I dearly wanted my birth father to walk me down the aisle and for him to give me away, as any natural-born daughter would have done.

However, Miss Y informed me that my father had refused to attend as he had just wanted to get on with his current life. This upset me considerably. It transpires that the truth was that he desperately wanted to attend but had been told quite forcefully that he would not have been made welcome!

I cringed walking down the aisle before being given away by Macaw, having to hold his arm, pretending to the world that all was ok.

Many years later, on the occasion of our 30th wedding anniversary, my father did attend the celebrations and, having been invited to make a speech, said how happy he was to have had the opportunity to put things right and to set the record straight, adding how proud he was of his daughter.

I love my husband, but I still look over my shoulder due to my experiences.

I have always been exceptionally protective of my marriage and towards our children and grandchildren but also any other children, following on from my very nasty experiences. Some, I am sure would say overprotective perhaps.

The relationship between me and my husband is genuine, romantic and we are still very much in love and faithful to each other.

The only person that Miss Y loved was herself and a word that isn't and never was in her vocabulary is *'faithful'.*

Like many victims in similar situations, I closed my mind and buried what had happened in my subconscious but occasional triggers would create unwanted recollections. It was not until a few years after my marriage that I finally plucked up the courage to mention to my husband some of the events that had occurred whilst I had been living at *The Lair and* then with his support, summoned up enough courage to go public with the information.

Even then, I was only able to give an abridged version, not out of dishonesty but simply because of my inner self suppressing some of the more awful memories of those painful days.

Unfortunately, Miss Y never seems to have ever changed her attitude. Even after I had left home, it always seemed to be a case of putting herself first. As recently as just over two years ago, my husband phoned Miss Y to tell her that I had been diagnosed with a lung condition and had long-term voice loss because of respiratory issues, partly as a result of having a lack of immune system. Instead of expressing any concern for me or even asking how I was, Miss Y interrupted and demanded to know from my husband why *she* had not been told about the then recent passing of my father, even though by then she had been divorced from him for well over 50 years as a result of her multiple affairs.

There was no mention of her sympathy being passed to me, even though I was still grieving the recent loss of my father!

Also, the way she went about finding out of my father's passing was despicable and selfish, by asking an acquaintance of hers to phone his widow, pretending to be an old friend, to ask how he was.

The fact that Miss Y had totally ignored my health situation just demonstrates the complete lack of care or interest in anyone else but herself.

I still have those same respiratory issues, but the only response from Miss Y following on from the incident has been to leave a voicemail on two separate occasions asking why I was no longer talking to her and *'Did I really want her to go to her grave without being in contact?'* – completely ignoring the fact that she knew about my voice loss and respiratory problems.

Although I have to be very careful with my health, we have a motor-home and this allows us to travel with on-board facilities for some respite and fresh air.

I cannot understand the negative attitude towards me from Miss Y.

All of her various crimes, drug involvement, and deviousness, as well as the actions of Macaw have only affected me negatively.

The past remains very much in the present, as bad memories surface of being a daughter by name only.

But being a survivor is a different thing altogether.

On the positive side, I am happily married to the very best husband and am fortunate to have two fantastic sons, two lovely daughters-in-law, and our grandchildren.

Being married to my husband who is kind, caring, and thoughtful, and has been very understanding and supportive over all that has happened has helped contribute to me in a positive way.

There have been a few sharp lessons for me at times, but I have learned from observing Miss Y and have vowed to never ever follow in her footsteps, as I could never do that to anyone.

I love my children and grandchildren and protect them whenever and wherever possible, as family means everything to both me and my husband.

As much as there may be some criticism of me for writing this book and going public with some of the comments, for every negative there must be more of a positive.

At the end of the day some of the information here has been supplied from the public domain, so is already out there if you know where to look.

It has just been highlighted by being published in a book with the remaining truth contained within it.

Despite me attempting on many occasions to have contact with her, Miss Y has just demonstrated more and more negativity towards me. She was never there for me as a parent should have been and I have slowly learned by watching her separate me from my sibling.

Roughly twenty years ago, one Christmas, Miss Y decided that she would turn the waterworks on and said to my sibling that I had been cruel and unkind to her.

This was untrue obviously but it gained the result Miss Y had wanted by turning my sister against me, and since then my sister has not communicated with me.

It has not been at all easy writing this book but when someone who should have been a maternal positivity in your life continuously 'grinds you down' and uses every opportunity to criticise you, eventually enough is enough and so this book needed to be written, not just for me but also for anyone else who might just be suffering either mentally, physically or sexually or a mixture of all at the hands of a relative or any other person, I can relate to you and can understand how you might be feeling.

Postscript

I am the author of this book.

To clarify — the three main characters in this book:

- *My grandfather;*
- *My mother, by birth only, who is known as Miss Y for the purpose of this book;*
- *Me, the author, and I am, as you may have guessed by now, Linda Knight.*

It has been extremely painful and raw narrating my experiences, but I sincerely hope that it will help other people who may have suffered similar actions.

Every penny of the profits from the sale of the book will be given to NAPAC, a charity that supports the victims of child abuse and, more importantly, the survivors of such attacks.

I am not a victim... I am a survivor.

Linda Knight